Mallorca
and Menorca

Berlitz
Mallorca
and Menorca

Text by Neil E. Schlecht
Photography: Neil E. Schlecht except pages 9, 12,
        39, 45, 76, 83, 87, 96 by Jon
        Davison
Cover Photo: Jon Davison
Photo Editor: Naomi Zinn
Layout by Media Content Marketing, Inc.
Cartography by Raffaele DeGennaro
Managing Editor: Tony Halliday

Fifth Edition 2002

CONTACTING THE EDITORS
Every effort has been made to provide accurate information in this publication, but
changes are inevitable. The publisher cannot be responsible for any resulting loss,
inconvenience or injury. We would appreciate it if readers would call our attention to
any errors or outdated information by contacting Berlitz Publishing, PO Box 7910,
London SE1 1WE, England. Fax: (44) 20 7403 0290;
e-mail: berlitz@apaguide.demon.co.uk

*Printed in Singapore by Insight Print Services (Pte) Ltd, 38 Joo Koon Road, Singapore
628990. Tel: (65) 6865-1600. Fax: (65) 6861-6438*

*Berlitz Trademark Reg. U.S. Patent Office and other countries. Marca Registrada.
Used under licence from the Berlitz Investment Corporation*

080/205 RP

CONTENTS

Fact Sheets

● A (☞ in the text denotes a highly recommended sight

Mallorca
and Menorca

THE ISLANDS AND THEIR PEOPLE

The Balearic Islands don't have to work too hard to embody the perfect island vacation. Mallorca and Menorca are blessed with the sort of natural and man-made attributes that entice countless millions of foreign visitors to descend upon them and to keep returning year after year: the perfect deep blue and transparent turquoise of the Mediterranean Sea, 300-plus days of brilliant annual sunshine, hundreds of miles of coastline, secluded coves and wide bays, and a vast choice of cheap flights and accommodations.

Since the 1960s, Mallorca has shone in its role as Spain's tourism juggernaut, defining the extremes of a Mediterranean holiday: the unbridled hedonism of topless beaches and singles bars, and the lethargic, point A (hotel) to point B (beach) vacation. Wealthy visitors to the island enjoy privileged holidays revolving around second homes, boating and sailing. The image was established early, and the cash registers have been ringing ever since.

But tourism pulls islanders in opposite directions on the Balearics. Income derived from a well-orchestrated travel industry has made this region Spain's wealthiest per capita, but the environmental and psychological effects of being Europe's playground have left locals a bit desperate. Four decades after it exploded, tourism on the islands overheated, leaving in its ashes a forest of massive, block-booked hotels and beach-hugging villa communities with few discernible ties to Spain—places lined with German *bier* halls, English fish 'n' chips joints, and low-rent bars and discos.

At a time when countries are going to new extremes battling for their share of the world tourism pie, Mallorca and

Menorca are reassessing their enduring popularity. Fearing that overdevelopment, as well as new trends and tastes in international tourism, would leave the Balearics behind, authorities have moved to protect remaining undeveloped areas as nature preserves, proclaiming them off-limits to all construction, and have even blown up some of the more unsightly hotel blemishes on the coasts.

The people and governments of Mallorca and Menorca have recognized a need to choose between surrendering the natural beauty and easygoing lifestyle of their islands to the ravenous consumption of foreign vacationers and homebuyers, and protecting what's left of each. Happily, there's still a lot that hasn't yet been adulterated on the two islands—meaning that visitors also have a choice. They can join hordes of their sun-deprived brethren from Great Britain, Germany, and other countries, and enjoy an island vacation with a cheap place to stay, familiar food, glorious beaches, and a few day excursions thrown in for variety. The summer season grows longer every year, and significant stretches of both islands are still packed with merrymakers and families delighting in the traditional Mediterranean island vacation.

Or if that thought is less appealing to you, though, as it is to increasing numbers of travelers, you'll find another side to the Balearics. It is more chic than cheap, a place where ecologically sensitive hotels are built in restored 16th-century manor and farm houses, where hiking, cycling, and golf complement or replace entirely the long days at the beach. It is place to eat fine Mallorcan, Menorcan, and Spanish cuisine rather than pizza and French fries.

Incredibly, tiny Mallorca has Spain's largest and busiest airport. Son Sant Joan, Palma de Mallorca's international airport, pulls in about 7 million visitors annually—approximately 11 times the island's year-round population.

This "other" Balearics may not be as inexpensive or as accessible as the one sold by travel operators, but if visitors venture beyond the well-trodden tracks of their packaged predecessors, they'll discover a spectacularly beautiful part of the world. If you come expecting a nightmarish land of charter flights, tour buses, and beer-stained beach hangouts, you may be shocked at how remote and undeveloped many parts of these small islands remain. From medieval mountain villages and the dramatic lunar landscape of Mallorca's Formentor promontory to mysterious prehistoric settlements and isolated beaches accessible only by foot on Menorca, the islands abound with sights that are anything but blandly international.

The simple life — A Port de Sóller fisherman repairs his nets in the sun.

Slowly but surely, visitors are graduating from sterile hotels and apartment blocks to home rentals, time shares, and *casas rurales*—"country house" hotels that form part of the government's agrotourism initiatives. No longer the sole habitat of sun worshippers, the islands welcome thousands of cyclists in early spring; April and May bring hikers to exclaim over wildflowers; and bird-watchers with binoculars and zoom lenses record rarities and migrants on their way north.

Previous generations moved inland to get out of range of marauding pirates. Islanders who stayed put, and didn't flee to the coast to work the tourism industry, can live almost unmolested by beach-bound modern invaders. Against the odds, much of the islands' traditional life and values has been preserved, and while agriculture is no longer the dominant income source, plenty of people still have little connection to tourism. This is especially true on Menorca, where cold winter winds limit the season's length.

Mallorca, the largest of the four Balearics, is also the most geographically varied. The dramatic cliffs of the Serra de Tramuntana mountain range hug the coastline of the entire northwest and north, from Andratx all the way to the Cape of Formentor. The north coast boasts some of Spain's most stunning scenery: miniscule coves, dizzying drops to the sea, picturesque medieval villages, and a sin-

Morning glory — A sunrise of pinks and golds at the harbor of Palma, Mallorca's cosmopolitan, photogenic capital.

gle port, at Sóller. The interior of Mallorca is a vast plain of small industrial towns, farmlands, and ancient, gnarly olive and almond trees, all protected from Mediterranean winds by the rugged mountains. The south is dominated by the cosmopolitan island capital, Palma de Mallorca, its handsome bay, and the crowded beaches that splay outward from it. The east coast is an enticing mix of bays, long sweeps of beach, small coves, spectacular caves, and myriad tourist villas.

Menorca is the second largest of the Balearic archipelago, but it's tiny just the same: only 50 km (31 miles) long and 17 km (10 miles) across at its widest point. Predominantly rural and flat, Menorca has always been a quieter place than Mallorca (or the craziest of the Balearics, partymad Ibiza). Still, its hidden coves, remarkable natural harbors, and more than 1,000 Megalithic monuments — inscrutable remnants of the island's prehistoric origins — are dazzling. Menorca gets big-time package holidaymakers, especially from Great Britain, and beaches and roads get awfully crowded in the height of the summer season, but the island seldom feels frenetic.

With all these things going for them, including a friendly, easygoing population conversant in several languages, it's not surprising that the Balearics continue to reel in short- and long-term visitors by the millions. Many northern Europeans, especially Germans, have purchased sum-

Linguistic Stew

The local languages are dialects of Catalan, called Mallorquí and Menorquí. Spanish (Castilian) is used universally, especially in business and in dealings with Spain. English and German, the languages of real estate deals and tourism, are also widely understood.

mer and retirement homes here; during the months of July and August, Spaniards are flatly outnumbered, when the dominant languages are German and English. In parts of Mallorca, Germans own about 80 percent of all homes; along traditionally British vacation spots on Menorca, three-quarters of the homes are first or second residences belonging to the English. Understandably, locals' patience can get a bit frayed by the end of summer. It is being tested further as more visitors buy into the old towns and villages, instead of just coastal resorts.

But foreign invasions are nothing new to these islanders. They were conquered successively by Carthaginians, Romans, Vandals, Christians, and Moors. Slightly less possessive but equally curious visitors arrived, including the lovers George Sand and Frédéric Chopin, Archduke Louis Salvator of Austria, Anaïs Nin, and the poet Robert Graves. The islands are now invaded by modern royalty like Claudia

Schiffer, Michael Douglas, as well as princes and their paramours who anchor their yachts in the ports and evade the paparazzi. Many islanders have learned to regard the latest occupations with a sense of dry humor. All the previous occupiers have come and eventually gone, they say, and these too will one day leave.

Placid, hidden coves make Menorca an unforgettable island idyll.

A BRIEF HISTORY

Humans inhabited the Balearic archipelago as early as 5000 B.C., having most likely journeyed to the islands from the coast of mainland Spain. Neolithic islanders lived in caves and rock shelters, examples of which can still be seen on both Mallorca and Menorca, and hunted the only large animal on the islands, a type of mountain goat, now extinct. Many of the Balearic Islands are strewn with rocks and boulders, and these early peoples built simple stone houses and cleared fields by piling the stones into dividing walls.

Another skill with stones was evident in the islanders' deadly use of the sling, which brought them onto the world stage and into written history. Indeed, the name Balearic may come from the Greek *ballein*, "to throw." The Carthaginians absorbed the islands into their trading empire and founded the main ports, but they quickly learned to respect the slingers, eventually recruiting thousands into their armies. By 123 B.C. the Romans had pacified most of Spain and sent out an invading force. Having conquered the islands, they named them *Balearis Major (Mallorca) and Balearis Minor (Menorca)*.

The Romans built roads and established towns, including the towns of Palmaria (Palma) and Pollentia (near present-day Alcúdia). In the fifth century, as the Empire crumbled, tribes called barbarians by the Romans — Goths, Vandals and Visigoths — poured into Spain. The Vandals, who destroyed almost all evidence of the Roman occupation, settled in North Africa, becoming a sea power. A Byzantine expedition from Constantinople ousted the Vandals from the Balearics in 534.

The Tide of Islam

Ignited in the Arabian peninsula by the teachings of the Prophet Muhammad, Islam spread like wildfire, with its

Turbulent times — Crenellated battlements of the 14th-century castle of Capdepera recall a history of invasion.

armies reaching the Atlantic coast of Morocco by 683. Determined to impose their new religion in Europe, a predominantly Moorish army led by the Arab general Tarik landed on the Iberian peninsula in 711. In just seven years nearly all of Spain was under Moorish rule.

The Muslim world, which reached from Baghdad to the Pyrenees, soon fragmented, with Spain becoming an independent caliphate. Under tolerant rulers, the capital city Córdoba was transformed into one of Europe's greatest centers of scholarship and the arts. At first the caliphs were content to accept tribute from the Balearics, without imposing Islam. But by 848 disturbances in the islands prompted the Moors to deploy their newly expanded navy; the Emir of Córdoba conquered both Mallorca and Menorca at the beginning of the tenth century. By the 11th century, the caliphate had splintered into a mosaic of fractious states — 26 at one point, and the Balearics became an independent emirate.

The Reconquest

The aim of the Crusades in Spain was the eviction of the Muslims. After the recovery of Jerusalem in 1099, it took four hundred years of sieges and battles, treaties, betrayals, and yet more battles, before Christian kings and warlords succeeded in subduing the Moors.

On 10 September 1229, a Catalan army led by King Jaume I of Aragón and Catalunya took the Mallorcan shore near the present-day resort of Santa Ponça. The defenders retreated inside the walls of Palma, but on the last day of 1229 the city fell, and pockets of resistance throughout the island were also defeated. Jaume I proved to be an enlightened ruler who profited from the talents of the Moors — converted by force to Christianity — as well as of the island's large Jewish and Genoese trading communities. Mallorca prospered.

The Moors on Menorca speedily agreed to pay an annual tribute to Aragón and were left in peace. The island's tranquility lasted until 1287, when Alfonso III of Aragón, smarting over a series of humiliations at the hands of his nobles, found a pretext for invasion. The Moors were defeated and expelled or killed. In contrast to Mallorca, Menorca's economy was devastated for decades.

Jaume I died after reigning in Aragón for six decades, but he made the cardinal error of dividing between his sons the lands he had fought for so long to unite. At first this resulted in an Independent Kingdom of Mallorca, under Jaume II, followed by Sanç and Jaume III. But family rivalry triggered the overthrow of Jaume III by his cousin Pedro IV, who then seized the Balearics for Aragón. Attempting a comeback, Jaume was killed in battle near Llucmajor in 1349.

A newly unified Christian Spain under the Catholic Monarchs, Ferdinand and Isabella, completed the Reconquest, defeating the only Moorish enclave left on the Iberian peninsula, Granada, in 1492. However, the centralized kingdom failed to incorporate the Balearics politically or economically.

The Spanish Empire

As one tumultuous age ended, one of glory and greed began. Christopher Columbus, the seafaring captain from Genoa (whom at least three Mallorcan towns claim as their own) believed he could reach the East Indies by sailing westwards. In the same year that Granada fell, Columbus crossed the Atlantic, landing in the Caribbean islands.

Spain exported its adventurers, traders, and priests, and imposed its language, culture, and religion on the New World, creating a vast empire in the Americas. Ruthless, avaricious *conquistadores* extracted and sent back incalculable riches of silver and gold. The century and a half after 1492 has been called Spain's "Golden Age." However, the era carried the seeds of its own decline. Plagued by corruption and incompetence, and drained of manpower and ships by such adventurism as the dispatch of the ill-fated Armada against England in 1588, Spain was unable to defend her expansive interests. Burgeoning trade in the Balearics was interrupted by marauding pirates based in North Africa as well as by the powerful Turkish fleet.

French and British Ties and Occupation

The daughter of Ferdinand and Isabella married the son and heir of the Holy Roman Emperor, Maximilian of Hapsburg. The Spanish crown duly passed to the Hapsburgs, and Spain remained in their hands until the feeble-minded Carlos II died in 1700, leaving no heir. France seized the chance to install the young grandson of Louis XIV on the Spanish throne.

A rival Hapsburg claimant was supported by Austria and Britain, who saw a powerful Spanish-French alliance as a major threat. In the subsequent War of the Spanish Succession (1702–1713) most of the old kingdom of Aragón, including the Balearics, backed the Hapsburgs. Britain seized Gibraltar — in the name of the Hapsburg claimant — and retained it when the war was over. In 1708 Britain captured Menorca, and the magnificent harbor of Mahón (Maó), for the Royal Navy. England clung to it even when Bourbon forces captured Mallorca at the end of the war.

Palma's Arab baths — in early Balearic history, the Moors reigned supreme.

Menorca changed hands between Britain, France, and Spain five more times in less than a century. Britain finally ceded the island to Spain in the year 1802, under the terms of the Treaty of Amiens.

By 1805, Spain was once more aligned with France, and Spanish ships fought alongside the French against Nelson at Trafalgar. Napoleon came to distrust his Spanish ally and forcibly replaced the king of Spain with his own brother, Joseph Bonaparte. A French army marched in to subdue the country. The Spanish resisted and, aided by British troops commanded by the Duke of Wellington, drove the French out. What British historians call the Peninsular War (1808–1814) is known in Spain as the War of Independence.

In the 19th century, practically all of Spain's possessions in the Americas broke away in the wake of the

Napoleonic Wars, and the few that remained were lost at the end of the 19th century. The Balearics, further neglected, were beset with poverty and outbreaks of disease. However, toward the 20th century, things began to improve on the islands, with Mallorca reaping the rewards of successful agricultural crops and Menorca launching an export shoe industry.

The beginning of the 20th century in Spain was marked by still more crises, assassinations, and near anarchy. The colonial war in Morocco provided an almost welcome distraction, but a disastrous defeat there in 1921 led to a coup in which the general Primo de Rivera became dictator. The dictator fell in 1929, and when the elections of 1931 revealed massive anti-royalist feeling in Spain's cities, the king followed him into exile.

The Republic and Civil War

The new republic was conceived amid an orgy of strikes, church-burnings, and uprisings of the right and left. In Feb-

Ancient creep right up to the edge of the bay of Palma. For centuries, the Balearics have been coveted and conquered.

ruary 1936 te left-wing Popular Front won a majority of seats in the *Cortes*, but across Spain new extremes of violence displaced argument.

In July 1936, most of the army, led by General Francisco Franco — with the support of the monarchists, conservatives, the clergy, and the right-wing Falange — rose against the government in Madrid. Aligned on the government's side were the Republicans, including liberals, socialists, Communists, and anarchists. The ensuing Spanish Civil War was brutal and bitter, and support for both sides poured in from outside Spain. Many saw it as a contest between democracy and dictatorship, or, from the other side, between order and Red chaos. Fascist Italy and Nazi Germany backed Franco's Nationalists, while the Soviet Union supported the Republicans (although less and less towards the end of the war). Volunteers from Britain and the US arrived to fight on the side of the Republicans. The war lasted three years; perhaps one million Spaniards lost their lives.

Mallorca and Menorca found themselves on opposite sides during the war. Menorca declared itself for the republic, and stayed with it to the bitter end. Mallorca's garrison seized it for Franco's Nationalists. Early in the war, the Republicans used their one battleship to support an invasion of Mallorca, but it ended in failure. A decisive factor was the presence in Palma of Italian air squadrons, used to bomb republican Barcelona.

New Horizons

Exhausted after the Civil War, Spain remained on the sidelines during World War II and began to recover economically under the oppressive, law-and-order regime of Franco. There had been a foretaste of elite foreign tourism in the 1920s, but it was the late 1950s when the rest of Europe began sun-seeking pilgrimages to Spain. Tourism exploded into an annual southern migration, transforming the Spanish economy, landscape, and society. Eager to capitalize, the country poured its soul into mass tourism, which triggered a rash of indiscriminate building on the southern and eastern coastlines, with scant regard for tradition or aesthetics. But after so many years closed off from the rest of Europe, of equal significance was the injection of foreign influences into Franco's once hermetically sealed Spain. Mallorca and Menorca in particular saw explosive growth in tourism; by the 1970s, the Balearics were one of Europe's most popular holiday destinations.

Franco named as his successor the grandson of Alfonso XIII, who was enthroned as King Juan Carlos I when the dictator died in 1975. To the dismay of Franco diehards, the king brilliantly managed the transition to democracy, then stood back to allow it full rein, even intervening during a brief attempt at a military coup. After many years of repression, new freedoms and autonomy were granted to Spanish regions, including the Balearics, and their languages and cultures enjoyed a long-desired renaissance.

More a part of Europe than ever before, Spain joined the European Community (now European Union) in 1986, giving further boost to a booming economy. The tourist industry continued to expand, and though it became one of the top two income earners in Spain, a realization that unrestricted mass tourism was leading to damaging long-term consequences also began to grow. By the late 1990s, a new emphasis on quality and, especially in the Balearics, on safeguarding the environment had finally taken root—too late for many environmentalists, but hopefully still in time to preserve much of the natural beauty and unique character of the *Las Islas Baleares*.

HISTORICAL LANDMARKS

5000 B.C. First evidence of human habitation in the Balearics.

1300 B.C. Megalithic culture called Talaiotic reigns, especially on Menorca; great stone towers called talaiots first constructed.

700 B.C.–400 B.C. Carthaginians conquer and colonize the Balearics.

123 B.C. Romans defeat Carthaginians in Balearics and name individual islands Balearis Major (Mallorca) and Balearis Minor (Menorca).

120 B.C.–A.D. 400 Romans consolidate Balearics into empire, found towns, including Palmaria (Palma) and Pollentia (Alcúdia) on Mallorca and Port Magonum (Maó) on Menorca.

A.D. 426 Vandals invade Balearics.

711 Moorish invasion forces land near Gibraltar, and Spain eventually falls under Islamic rule.

848 Caliphs of Spain quell disturbances in the Balearics and impose Islam; Moorish rule in the Balearics to last 300 years.

1229 Palma falls to the Christian army, ending Moorish rule in Mallorca. Menorca agrees to pay tribute to Aragón.

1276 Jaume II crowned in Mallorca.

1285–1287 Alfonso III of Aragón captures Palma and invades Menorca.

1349 Jaume III killed in battle by Pedro IV of Aragón, ending the independent kingdom of Mallorca.

1492 Spain united under Ferdinand and Isabella.

1708 Menorca taken by the British; ceded to Spain in 1802.

1936–1939 Spanish Civil War. Menorca declares for the republic; Mallorca seized by Franco's Nationalist forces.

1975 King Juan Carlos I enthroned after death of Franco.

1986 Spain joins the European Community (now EU).

WHERE TO GO

Whether you're in Palma, a coastal resort, or an inland village, you can reach any point on Mallorca in half a day, and Menorca is even smaller and more concentrated. On both islands, tour companies offer excursions by road or in combinations with boat trips, to see the mountain and coastal scenery, famed beaches, spectacular caves, and various purpose-built attractions. At these sights, though, you'll invariably be part of a crowd, especially in high season (which grows every year). Accommodations are also at a premium from July through September. Charter flights and package deals (hotel and airfare) become considerably more economical if you're willing to visit in the shoulder or off season.

Hiring a car (see page 104) is the ideal way to see Mallorca and Menorca, allowing you to go where you like — some of the least-known places are the most delightful. You can get around by public bus, with a couple of trains thrown in, but those options won't allow you to see as much in a short time.

The great majority of visitors enter the Balearics through its capital, Palma de Mallorca (and in fact, most stay within 20 km (13 miles) or so of the city, ensconced in seaside hotels and villas). Any thought you might have had that you would be vacationing in a sleepy Mediterranean island backwater will quickly be dashed upon arrival at sprawling Son Sant Joan, Palma de Mallorca's international airport.

As islands go, Mallorca is quite large: it has more than 550 km (325 miles) of coastline and is, at its widest, 100 km (60 miles) across. Visiting all the major regions of Mallorca with any degree of seriousness would require several weeks, while most of much-smaller Menorca can be seen in a week's time. On a short holiday, it's best to choose a couple of regions and take them in at a relaxed pace. See the list of beach highlights on pages 82 and 85.

PALMA DE MALLORCA

Palma is a large, cosmopolitan, working city, with a population that accounts for two-thirds of the permanent population of Mallorca. Yet the city feels undeniably tropical and sensual. This has something to do with the palm trees, relentless sunshine, yachts bobbing in the bay, and fishermen laying out their nets on the waterfront, to be sure, but it's also a product of the way locals talk, walk, dress, and sip wine and coffee at outdoor cafés. Their leisurely manner tells you this is no mainland capital.

Palma dominates the island — a glance at the map shows how the island's road system radiates from the city — but it is a world far removed from the mountain villages of the northwest, the small towns of the interior, and the tourist-ruled coastal villas. The area of greatest interest to visitors is

Mallorca's pride: The gorgeous city of Palma, with its splendid Gothic cathedral perched above the bay.

the small old quarter that surrounds the cathedral, which sits on a small hill overlooking the bay. Historic Palma can be seen in a day or two, though the plazas, cafés, restaurants, and bars may cause you to linger.

From the harbor the great Gothic cathedral rises on a small hill and dominates the center of the city, with the ancient Almudaina Palace immediately below it. To the east is Platja de Palma, a long line of excellent sandy beaches that have been defaced by a sad stretch of concrete from Ca'n Pastilla to S'Arenal; to the west is the elegant seaside promenade, Passeig Marítim, of modern Palma, where luxury hotels look out over a forest of masts in the yacht harbor. Crowning the wooded slopes above it are the stone towers of Bellver Castle.

The Romans established a strategic post near where Palma now stands so gracefully, but the Moors were primarily responsible for transforming the site into a real city. Few Arab buildings remain, having been razed during the Reconquest, but the old quarter (*Centre Historic* on direction signs) still abounds with buildings of historic interest, preserved when Palma fell into decline in the 16th and 17th centuries. The old city's narrow, atmospheric streets are full of pleasant surprises, best seen on foot.

☞ The focus of any visit to Palma is, justifiably, its massive Gothic **Cathedral** — one of the finest churches in Spain. Called *La Seu* by locals, it was begun in 1230, after the Christians recaptured the island from the Moors. King Jaume made an emphatic political point by ordering it built on the site of the Great Mosque. Building was slow and sporadic, affected by wars and finance, and the great work took nearly four centuries to complete. Densely packed buttresses facing seaward create an extraordinary effect of power and beauty, especially when they blaze like gold in the setting sun and cast their reflection in the pool below. Before entering, have a look at the remarkable **Portal del Mirador** entrance, overlooking Palma's bay. The 14th-century door is a feast of carved stone figurines, including a depiction of the Last Supper by Guillem Sagrera. The north door of the cathedral, near the 13th-century bell tower, is reserved for those attending religious services in the early morning and early evening. Tourists are encouraged to visit the cathedral in conjunction with the **Cathedral Museum** next door, a treasure-trove of silver monstrances and candelabra, saintly relics, Gothic paintings, and Baroque altars. A colossal and ornate early Renaissance doorway in carved stone leads on to the oval New Chapter House. From the museum, one enters the cathedral.

The wrought-iron Crown of Thorns canopy over the high altar (called the Baldachino) was added by the Catalan *modernista* architect Antoni Gaudí at the beginning of the 20th century. Gaudí, who worked some 10 years on the cathedral, also moved the choir stalls from the central nave.

On the west side of the cathedral is the **Palau de l'Almudaina**, once the royal residence of the Moorish rulers. Part of the palace is open to visitors, and a short tour takes in a stone-vaulted 13th-century throne room, divided into two stories in the 16th century — you'll see

Cathedral "La Seu," one of the most remarkable churches in all of Spain.

that the window was cut off in the process. In the heavily restored royal offices, which are used by the present king and queen, traces of early paintwork survive on ceilings and frescoed walls. There are also several impressive 15th- and 16th-century Flemish tapestries.

Leafy **Passeig des Born**, the elongated plaza that runs inland, is where locals love to take their early evening promenade. Once the site of jousting tournaments, it's now lined with park benches and cafés. At no. 27 is an 18th-century Italianate mansion, **Casa Solleric,** which today houses a cultural foundation and hosts art exhibitions.

In the narrow streets behind the cathedral are tall houses, several of which are **baronial mansions** dating from the 15th and 16th centuries, with dark walls and great wooden doors. Their forbidding exteriors hide some of Palma's most inviting courtyards, which can be glimpsed through the heavy metal grilles. The **Can Bordils** on carrer Almudaina retains its Gothic architecture; **Can Oms**, at number 7, is an 18th-century noble house with one of Palma's finest patios. Crossing over carrer Almudaina is the ancient Arab arch, **Arc de L'Almudaina**. Many courtyards were remodeled in the 17th and 18th centuries, including **Casa Olesa** (carrer Morey, 9), with its cool, wide-arched patios, balconies and stately staircases. Other spectacular mansions are nearby on carrer Can Savellà; look for the the Baroque **Can Vivot** (sometimes called Can Sureda) at number 4 and **Can Catlar del Llorer,** with its Gothic patio built in the 13th century, at number 15.

On carrer de la Portella, a palatial Renaissance mansion has been restored as the somewhat sleepy **Museu de Mallorca**. Descriptions are only in Catalan, but the relics of the Muslim period and fine 13th- to 15th-century paintings and carvings, originally from Palma's churches, antique tiles and ceramics, and a display of *modernista* furniture on the top floor make the

museum worth a visit. The top floor also houses exhibitions by present-day Mallorcan artists. Old photographs show some of the Arab gateways that were destroyed when the city walls were razed in 1902. The **Banys Àrabs** (Arab Baths), behind the museum on carrer de Can Serra, 7, are miraculously still standing after 1,000 years.

The 13th-century **Basílica de Sant Francesc** (Basílica of St. Francis), on the Plaça Sant Francesc, is one of Palma's treasures. A statue of Junípero Serra, the 18th-century founder of the first Franciscan missions in

Street action — the hustle and bustle of a busy Mallorcan plaça makes for a fun stroll.

California, is erected in front of the Plateresque carved portal. Inside the church lies the sarcophagus of the 13th-century sage and scholar Ramón Llull. He and Serra are two of Mallorca's greatest sons and heroes — they have both been beatified, and sainthood seems sure to follow. The church is rather dark and heavy, a real contrast with the enchanting cloisters, whose slender double columns and stone tracery are light and delicate.

The **Plaça Cort** is the site of the fine wooden-eaved 17th-century Renaissance Ajuntament (Town Hall) and from there it's a short way by smart shopping streets to the yellow façades and green shutters of the **Plaça Major**, the former marketplace. On the west side of the Plaça Major is Plaça de Marqués Palmer; sandwiched among chic leather and footwear shops are two ex-

Built in 1903 the imposing Gran Hotel was the first modern hotel in Mallorca.

cellent examples of *modernista* (Catalan Art Nouveau) architecture: **Can Forteza Rei** and **L'Àguila**, whose iron grill work and broken-tile flourishes are similar to better-known modernista buildings found in Barcelona.

Down the steps that lead to the Plaça Major is Plaça Weyler (off of carrer Unió), where there are two more fine examples of *modernisme*. One is the imposing and ornate former **Gran Hotel**. The first modern hotel in Mallorca, it was built in 1903 by Lluís Doménech i Muntaner, the architect responsible for Barcelona's wondrous Palau de la Música concert hall. Across from the Gran Hotel is a small bakery, the **Forn des Teatre**, whose modernista decoration graces many a postcard in Palma. Down the street, next to Plaça Mercat, is **Can Casayas,** two more gently undulating modernista buildings.

Back near the waterfront, the turreted **Sa Llotja** (La Lonja in Spanish) was built in the mid-15th century by local architect Guillem Sagrera (the seafront promenade is named after him). Once the city merchants' stock exchange (now used to house art exhibitions — the only time it can be visited), it is one of Spain's finest civic Gothic buildings. Slim columns twist through its light and airy interior to the vaulted roof. Next to

Sa Llotja, a cannon and an anchor surround the 17th-century **Consolat de Mar**, the former maritime law court — now the seat of the Balearic Islands' autonomous government.

When the evening promenade disperses, the streets of the old city are usually quiet, dark, and practically deserted, though the small streets between Plaça de La Llotja and Plaça la Reina teem with restaurants and bars. There is still more action if you head west to **Es Jonquet**, once the fishermen's quarter, now full of bars, cafés, and clubs clustering under the old windmills which used to grind the city's flour.

A few hundred meters inland from Es Jonquet, the **Poble Espanyol** is a rather kitschy walled town of scaled-down replicas of Spanish architectural treasures from across Spain, including Granada's famed Alhambra palace. The buildings house shops, craft studios, bars, and cafés.

Just south of the Poble Espanyol, perched on a hilltop amid pine trees and parkland, is the fine **Castell de Bellver** (Bellver Castle). A magnificent example of Gothic military architecture, the castle has commanded the sea and land approaches to the city since its construction in the early 14th century by order of King Jaume II. The view from the circular battlements of the city and Bay of Palma is stunning. Notice how the sloping roof funneled rainwater into the castle's cisterns. Inside, there's a small, well-laid-out museum of the archaeology of the area.

THE BAY OF PALMA

Two magnificent sweeps of white sand almost 30 km (19 miles) long made Palma's bay a summertime people-magnet, and the resorts that mushroomed along them gave Mallorca a name for cheap and cheerful holidays in the 1960s and '70s. In recent years, the picture has turned decidedly boozy and tacky. Athough the coast around Palma is dominated by down-market package tourism, there are pockets of luxurious and expensive tourist villas.

East: Platja de Palma

The southeastern shore of the bay runs through former fishing villages to the beach resort and yacht harbor of **Ca'n Pastilla,** almost at the end of the airport runway. Then come **Sometimes, Las Maravillas**, and **S'Arenal**, on a 7-km (4-mile) strip of hotels, fast food restaurants, high-throttle bars and discos, British pubs, and German beerhalls. By day you'll have to pick your way across the beach through a sea of tightly packed bodies — despite the inconveniences, **Platja de Palma** is an outstanding long (4.5 km/2.8 miles) stretch of white sand.

West Side of the Bay

To the west of Palma, **Cala Major** ("great cove") was a holiday center long before the package-tour boom. The Catalan surrealist painter Joan Miró was a longtime resident of this

The bay of Palma strikes a serene pose with boats bobbing in its marina and the majestic cathedral looking on.

area, and the **Fundació Pilar i Joan Miró** displays a fine selection of his work, as well as his studio as he left it, and his living quarters. The coast, a mix of rocks and sand, continues west, past exclusive **Bendinat** up to **Portals Nous**, where apartment blocks cluster on the slopes. The glamorous-looking marina of **Puerto Punta Portals** is not natural but ambitiously carved out of the cliffs.

Sandy beaches start again at **Costa d'En Blanes** and **Palma Nova**, which morphs into big, brash, and overwhelmingly British **Magalluf**. The wide and sandy beach, sloping safely into the sea, is a solid block of bronzing bodies in summer. If you're looking for a bit of tourism overkill, this is where you'll find it: bars a block long, discos built like airport terminals, restaurants offering menus in eight languages from Finnish to French, waterslides, go-karts — you name it, Magalluf has it. Everything but sanity.

To the south, the once-quiet cove of **Cala Vinjes** (*kah*-la *veen*-juhs) has been practically buried in an orgy of concrete. Head for cover by continuing on through pine woods to narrow winding lanes to the pretty coves and beaches of **Portals Vells** (pohr-*tahls* vays). In the cliffs, you'll find huge rock-cut caverns dating from Roman times or earlier, enlarged over the centuries. Boats make the short excursion from the pier on Magalluf beach (meaning it's not always as peaceful as you might hope). Not far south of Portals Vells, you can hike to a very quiet cove, **Cala Figuera**. Farther on the road is blocked: the end of the peninsula is a military zone.

THE WESTERN TIP

The main road bypasses the resorts of the Bay of Palma and meets up with the sea once again at **Santa Ponça**, a modern villa that boasts one of the widest ranges of sports in

Mirador de Ricardo Roca, the first of a series of enticing coastline views heading north.

Mallorca and keeps going during the off season with an older clientele.

The pleasantly tree-shaded beaches of **Cala Fornells** are still picturesque, although hotels and clusters of Mexican *hacienda*-style villas press closely round. A scenic but twisting little road leads to **Port d'Andratx**, a broad, wonderfully sheltered bay that is home to more yachts than fishing boats these days. The old harbor area on the south side keeps its traditional appearance, though a closer look reveals a string of chic restaurants, and the slopes facing it across the water are encrusted with villas and apartments, most of which have now been bought up by wealthy Germans as second homes (Claudia Schiffer among them). Lack of a sandy beach has kept the big hotels away, which is just fine with most visitors. A short drive, brisk walk, or morning jog takes you 3 km (2 miles) to the **Cap de Sa Mola**, the most southwesterly point on the island, with its superb views of sheer cliffs and sparkling sea.

From in-land Andratx, a dead-end road leads to the coast at **Sant Elm**, a former fishing village that doesn't try too hard to be a resort. The view offshore from its mostly stony little beaches is dominated by the island of **Sa Dragonera**, said to look like a dragon rising from the sea, and subject of a long legal battle between would-be developers and conservationists. The green movement appears to have protected the odd-shaped island.

NORTHWEST: COAST AND MOUNTAINS

The most dramatic stretch of Mallorca's coastline looks across the Mediterranean to Barcelona. The rugged mountains of the Serra de Tramuntana sweep down to the sea so steeply here that there are few points of access and only one harbor and port of any size along the coast. The road winds along clifftops and the sea, providing a series of vertigo-inducing viewpoints, and meandering back into the mountains. Interspersed among the cliffs are terraced orchards, olive groves, and photogenic medieval villages. North of Andratx, the **coastal road C-710** reaches the first of a succession of *miradors*, lookout points with a commanding prospect of the entire coast. Some of them are still crowned with an ancient watchtower, from which lookouts anxiously scanned the sea for pirate ships and signaled warnings to the next point along the chain. If possible, make the trip early in the morning, or you'll be part of a procession from one parking spot to the next. The **Mirador de Ricardo Roca** provides enticing views of the coast looking north, but save some film, because they're even better a bit farther on.

Mind If I Borrow Your Piano?

Though Chopin was often ill during his stay in Valldemossa, he continued to compose, including his celebrated Raindrop Prelude. Chopin wrote the piece on a piano borrowed from the village, as his had been detained in customs — and didn't arrive until shortly before he was to leave Mallorca for good.

Four km (2½ miles) from the Roca lookout, **Estellencs** is a pretty, ancient town amid terraces and orange groves. From town you can walk or drive down a track to a little fishing cove. Back on the main road, some 5 km (3 miles) from Estellencs, take in perhaps the finest view of the entire coast — quite an accolade — from the snail-shaped 16th-century tower of the **Mirador de Ses Ànimes**. Green cliffs tumble into the stunningly blue Mediterranean far as the eye can see on either side. The next town's name is clearly Arabic in origin, and in fact the hillsides around **Banyalbufar** have been tamed since Moorish times into some of the finest (and most photographed) terraces on the island. Banyalbufar ("little vineyard by the sea") has a pair of pleasant hotels and several restaurants, making it a good place to spend the night. A small lane twists down to a rocky cove and small beach, while another reaches the sea at **Port d'es Canonge**.

North of Banyalbufar, the road turns inland for a while. Just off the road, in the direction of Esporles, you'll find **La Granja**, a popular tourist attraction and good family stop that is part stately home, part *finca* (traditional farmhouse), and part craft center.

The town of **Valldemossa** was transformed by the short visit, over a century and a half ago, of French writer George Sand and her lover, Frédéric Chopin. Their few weeks here in the winter of 1838–1839 seem to have been fairly miserable: Chopin was unwell, the weather was wet and cold and bad for his chest, and George Sand disparaged the villagers in her book *A Winter in Majorca*, calling them "barbarians and thieves." She nicknamed Mallorca "Monkey Island."

Now, busloads of visitors arrive daily in this picturesque mountain village to see the couple's lodgings in the former Carthusian monastery **La Cartuja**. The monks were expelled in 1835, and some of their cells were sold as holiday apartments. (The "cells" were in fact three-room suites with private gardens.) The two cells the lovers rented are now a museum, with original manuscripts, Chopin's death mask, and his piano. You'll see, too, the massive church, the monks' pharmacy with its collection of 18th-century jars, their library, and the guests' dining room.

In great contrast to George Sand's negative impressions of Mallorca was the lifelong love affair that the Austrian Archduke Ludwig Salvator (or Luis Salvador) had with the Balearics and their people. In 1870 he bought the estate of **Son Marroig** just outside Deià, which he proudly proclaimed the most beautiful place on earth. The house, open to visitors, is filled with his collections. In the gardens, take in the bird's-eye view from the cliff-edge temple built out of Italian marble. Hundreds of feet below the house is **Sa Foradada** (literally, "rock with a hole in it"), a rocky promontory jutting into the sea, pierced by a remarkable 18-m- (60-ft-) wide natural window. If you feel energetic, hop the little fence just south of Son Marroig and take the half-hour's walk down to the sea and the landing stage where the archduke Salvator used to anchor his yacht.

Archduke Ludwig Salvador proclaimed Son Marroig the most beautiful place on earth.

Nestled in the Tramuntana mountains, the village of Fornalutx is a veritable Mallorcan jewel.

Deià, a gorgeous hilltop town of honey-colored stone and brightly painted shutters just east of Son Marroig, has attracted plenty of artists and assorted expatriates ever since Robert Graves, the poet and author of *I, Claudius*, came to live here with Laura Riding in 1929. Graves was pursued by a strange coterie of admirers and late in life became the Grand Old Man of Deià, fierce in his defense of the northwest coast against touristic exploitation. He convinced the Minister of Tourism, a friend, to declare the area a nature reserve. The picture-perfect town is extremely popular in summer, when the year-round population of 613 swells with the trendy and chic who drive up rents by taking houses in Deià. Besides fancy luxury hotels in old manor houses, there are a couple of smart, low-cost alternatives, and one of the best rosters of restaurants on the coast, making Deià an ideal base for a few overnights. At the top of the village, near the church is a small cemetery overlooking the Mediterranean; a simple cement slab bears the inscription: *Robert Graves, Poeta, 1895–1985.*

It's a twisting 2-km (1-mile) drive down to Deià's tiny fishing cove (**Cala de Deià**), where ladder-like ramps come out of the boathouses set into the cliffs. A snack bar and a beach café open in summer, but the rocky shore can get choked with seaweed and tourists who'd hoped to find a private cove. Just beyond the turnoff to Cala de Deià is **Llucalcari**, which isn't properly signposted; look for the sign that says, simply, "Hotel" off to the left side of the road. The tiny village has but six or seven houses, several of them fortified with coats of armor emblazoned on the doors, but if you're up to an adventurous hike down the hill, hurdling a couple of gates property owners have installed to ward off crowds, you'll discover a rocky section of shoreline with pristine, transparent waters ideal for swimming.

At Sóller and its seaside twin **Port de Sóller**, the cliffs and mountains at last relent. The largest bay on the northwest coast makes a fine harbor, but both the water and the beach can be dirty. Sheltered slopes a few miles inland are covered in groves of lemon, orange, almond, and olive trees, with the island's highest mountain, **Puig Major** (1,445 m./4,740 ft), as a rugged backdrop. Sóller is a busy, prosperous town that claims, like several others, that it was the birthplace of Columbus. Sóller and Palma are linked by the narrow-gauge **Sóller Railway**, built in 1912. Five times a day (six on Sundays), polished wooden trains make the hour-long journey in each direction through orchards and spectacular mountain scenery, stopping at Son Sardina and Bunyola. The 10:40am *tren turístico* from Palma takes in an extra scenic halt above Sóller, allowing travelers to snap their shutters before moving on (otherwise, the trip is the same, except for the price).

In a valley of orange orchards and olive groves, **Sóller** is a compact little town of well-preserved 18th- and 19th-century mansions and agreeable churches and convents. The main square, Plaça Constitució, is a good place to idle for a while and absorb the appealing character of the town. A walk down Gran Vía reveals buildings with Art Nouveau and neo-Baroque flourishes, constructed during the town's early-20th-century expansion.

Two tiny and handsome villages near Sóller have enticed foreigners to acquire many of the medieval houses. ☞ **Fornalutx** is a jewel of warm stone so immaculate that it won a national prize a few years ago for spotlessness. Its steep cobblestone streets are lined with cacti and palm trees, and the Tramuntana mountains soar in the background. Similarly set among orange trees and wild flowers, **Biniaraix** is only a short stroll away down narrow lanes.

Authorities felt that the road from Palma to Sóller, with its hairpin bends and the 496-m (1,627-ft) pass, the Coll de Sóller, was impeding development. In spite of vigorous protests from environmentalists, plans were approved for a road tunnel under the mountains, and digging began in 1990. Travel time to Palma has been reduced to about a half-hour.

The drive from Sóller to Pollença looks short and easy on maps. It's neither. A beautiful, twisting road that hugs the Serra de Tramuntana, it has stunning views, but is for confident drivers. Almost no one makes the journey at night; after dark, it's advisable to drop down to Inca after Escorca and take the major (and straight and well-lit) highway east. You'll save time and your nerves.

On the southern slope, right opposite the tunnel entrance, are the **Jardins d'Alfabia,** a seigneurial mansion and gardens that were once the country estate of the Moorish Vizier of Palma. These days, the cisterns, fountains, and irrigation channels are a tad run down, but the flowing water and shaded walks, turkeys feeding under fig trees, and birds singing among exotic plants exude a gentle appeal. The house is like a forgotten palace, full of neglected treasures. Don't miss the huge wooden 14th-century oak chair in the print room, called by one expert "the most important antique in Mallorca."

Monasteri de Lluc, Mallorca's most revered place of pilgrimage.

The mountainous country to the east, reached via a lovely drive past Bunyola, is a favorite with hikers and walkers based at the tiny village of **Orient** or on daytrips from the coast. A massive mountain crag 822 m (2,700 ft) high is crowned by the **Castell d'Alaró**, a ruined fortress built by King Jaume I during the Moorish era. You can make the long walk from Orient, or drive most of the way to the summit up narrow and tortuous lanes, starting a little north of Alaró. The higher they climb, the rougher and narrower the tracks get (but most standard rental vehicles are capable of the trek). There's a restaurant and car park off to the left. The final ascent is on foot, up rocky paths; wear sturdy walking shoes. Look for the sign that reads *Castell a Peu* (To the castle on foot). It's a vigorous 30- to 45-minute climb. The gates and walls of the castle still guard the clifftop, and the views of the mountains and surrounding plains are as thrilling as any on Mallorca.

Forced away from the sea by the steep terrain, the main road north from Sóller climbs over the high pass of Coll de Puig Major — the **Mirador de Ses Barques** has fine views of the coast and Port de Sóller, as well as a restaurant — and past the dams and reservoirs of Cuber and Gorg Blau. Near the second dam, a little road leads to the coast. Its name, **Sa Calobra** ("the snake"), gives a hint of the 13 km (8 miles) of hairpin bends that have now become a tourist attraction in themselves; one loop is so exaggerated that the road passes under itself in a knot. Early morning is the best time to avoid the traffic (the most harrowing part of the descent is avoiding road-hogging, dangerous looking tourist buses). As a reward at the bottom of the winding road, Cala de Sa Calobra has a couple of restaurants, bars, and a pebbly beach, but all tend to be overcrowded with daytrippers. The main objective is the deep gorge of **Torrent de Pareis** ("the twins"). Tunnels, enlarged from natural crevices in the rock, burrow through to the riverbed where the gorge widens into a natural theater (concerts are given on some summer evenings).

At the **Monasteri de Lluc,** Mallorca's most revered place of pilgrimage, foreign visitors are for once frequently outnumbered by locals. The monastery, sequestered in a valley near the Puig des Castellot mountain, was founded in the 13th century, but the massive buildings you see today date from the 17th and 18th centuries. Islanders come to see and pray to a statue of the Madonna and Child, La Moreneta (or "little dark one"), so called because of its dark stone color. If you can attend mass in the church, you may hear the famous Lluc boys' choir, Es Blavets ("the blue ones"), named after the color of their cassocks. The monastery is a popular place with inexpensive accommodations, especially for hikers.

NORTHEAST: CAPES AND BAYS

The northwest coast isn't short on beauty or drama, but beaches are few and far between. Many visitors who seek beach time in Mallorca — a pretty reasonable desire, after all — beeline for the northeast coast and its two great sandy bays, which have picturesque mountainous backdrops and are within easy striking distance of the historic towns Pollença and Alcúdia, as well as the protected wetlands s'Albufera. The bays of Pollença and Alcúdia are lively and full of visitors, many of them families, during a long and hospitable summer season.

Pleasant **Port de Pollença** is the kind of place that, in contrast to much of the south, gives Mallorca a good name — with a perfectly sheltered, gently sloping sandy beach, a decent spectrum of hotels, *hostals*, apartments, and villas, good seafood restaurants, and relaxed nightlife options. Wedged in between two

Sheer cliffs and turquoise sea paint a picture of perfection at Cap de Formentor.

rocky promontories, it's a scenic place with luxury craft in the harbor and flotillas of windsurfers in the bay.

☞ Nearly every visitor to these parts ventures a bit farther northeast to the spectacular cliffs of **Península de Formentor**, the narrow headland jutting out 13 km (8 miles) on the north side of the bay. The best place to take in the extraordinary lunar landscape is the **Mirador de Mal Pas,** about 4 km (2½ miles) from Port de Pollença along an adventurous, twisting road. Sheer cliffs plunge dramatically to the Mediterranean, and the cape juts out to sea. Most boats and cars also stop at the pretty, pine-shaded beach (**Platja de Formentor**), a favorite spot for a picnic and swimming. The beach enjoys splendid views across the Badia de Pollença — the same you'd get with a night's stay at the exclusive Hotel Formentor, whose manicured gardens are visible from the beach.

From the turnoff to beach parking, it's another 6.5 km (4 miles) to the lighthouse out on **Cap de Formentor**. The road, swamped with cars, bicyclists, and tour buses, can be tortuous, as they all try to squeeze into the tiny parking lot at the top. As great as the views are, on a crowded day it may be advisable to turn off after 2.5 km (1½ miles) from the top. There you'll find a

Flex those calf muscles at Pollença's Via Crucis — 365 steps, 365 cypress trees.

single trek path down to **Cala Figuera**, a tiny cove with pierc-
ingly blue waters and a small beach framed by the rocky masses
of Formentor.

A few miles inland from the sea, **Pollença** was founded in
1230 after the defeat of the Moors. Until 1802 the town
belonged to the Order of the Knights of St. John, whose influ-
ence is evident in many handsome stone buildings in the center. The town has a tranquil, inviting atmosphere, especially
at the outdoor cafes of Plaça Major.

Whether Pollença's tiny bridge labeled *Pont Roman* is
really Roman is questionable, but the locals say so, and it
certainly looks the part. But the town's principal sight is the
Via Crucis (Way of the Cross), a long, steep climb of 365
steps, lined with 365 cypress trees, that lead to **El Calvari**
and the venerated church with a rhyming name, **Mare de
Déu del Peu de la Creu** (Mother of God at the Foot of the
Cross). If you're driving, there's also a road up, which passes the 14 Stations of the Cross.

One of the finest walks on Mallorca can be made only on
Saturdays. From Pollença, head north, taking the narrow
road towards **Ternelles**. Cars usually can go just a short distance before reaching a checkpoint where they have to turn
back. However, on Saturdays during spring and autumn the
landowners open their "frontier" to allow only walkers to go
through (even cyclists are prohibited). The route follows the
gorge of the Torrent de Ternelles at first, then turns off to

If you find yourself in northeast Mallorca on Good Friday,
head to Pollença. A figure of Jesus is dramatically carried
from El Calvari (Calvary Hill) down to Nostra Senyora dels
Àngels (Our Lady of the Angels), the church in Plaça
Major, the lower part of the city. The moving procession is
led by torchlight.

head for the ruined **Castell del Rei**, built by the Moors on a soaring crag 500 m (1,640 ft) above the sea. Another rough track leads down to the shore at Cala Castell. The entire hike is about 13 km (8 miles).

Between Pollença and Port de Pollença is the turnoff for **Cala Sant Vicenç**, a gleaming resort situated around three gorgeous sandy coves with brilliant blue water, excellent for swimming and snorkeling. The setting, framed by the craggy Serra de Comayaques and El Morral mountains, is spectacular — excellent for both families and day hikers.

Astride the neck of land between the Bay of Pollença and the even more expansive Bay of Alcúdia stands the ancient walled town of **Alcúdia**, first inhabited by the Phoenicians in the eighth century B.C. The Romans then built their capital, Pollentia, here. Too close to the sea for safety from raids, it must have depended on its impressive fortifications for protection (the massive walls you see today are mere imitations of the originals.) The sturdy Gothic church of Sant Jaume forms the southern bastion in the walls.

Beyond the road that circles the town you can see the low ruins remaining from Roman **Pollentia**. They're not impressive as such sites go, but some fine relics excavated here are now displayed in the little **Museu Monogràfic**, a nicely restored building opposite Sant Jaume church. Just off the road leading from Alcúdia to its port is the **Teatre Romà (Roman theater),** hewn out of solid rock in the first century B.C.

Port d'Alcúdia has evolved from a small fishing harbor into an all-purpose port for commercial, naval, and pleasure craft (there's a big yacht marina) and the largest summer resort in northern Mallorca. Restaurants and discos have multiplied, as have hotels and apartment blocks, which now spread around the bay to form an almost unbroken ribbon of buildings 10 km (6 miles) long. **Platja d'Alcúdia** in summer a solid block of bodies soaking up the sun. Though big and crowded, the resort remains pretty low-key, a good option for families with restless children.

Remarkably, so close to a major resort, lie the precious wetlands of **S'Albufera** are a haven for birdlife. Drainage plans in the 19th century ran into such problems that the British company responsible for a network of canals, paths, and bridges — still to be seen today — went bust. Much of the bay was originally surrounded by swampland, until development plans prompted large-scale reclamation. S'Albufera was one of the beneficiaries of the new environmental consciousness in Mallorca. You can now walk or cycle among the 800 hectares (2,000 acres) of wetlands and dunes that have been designated a *Parc Natural* (nature reserve), keeping a lookout for some of the more than 200 species of birds that have been spotted here.

The walled town of Alcúdia. First inhabited by the Phoenicians, the town then became the Roman capital, Pollentia.

EAST COAST: COVES AND CAVES

Mallorca's eastern coastline attracts nearly as many sun-seeking tourists as the extended Bay of Palma in the southwest. It's generally less seedy, if not much less crowded. Tiny harbors, some no more than a cleft in the cliffs, alternate with larger bays. Here and there, great clusters of villas are transformed from ghost town to boom town as soon as summer arrives.

Cala Ratjada is about as far as you can get from Palma without having to take to the water. But the water is what most people are here for, whether it's the fishermen, catamaran sailors, or the beach-bound vacationers. The resort is lively but undistinguished in appearance. Only the tourist information office (Tel. 971/56 30 33) can arrange a visit to the **Joan March Sculpture Garden**, on the grounds of the coastal mansion. March collected important works by Rodin, Henry Moore, Anthony Caro, and many modern Spanish masters.

Fine sandy beaches are close by at Cala Gat and Cala Moltó, though most of the bathers head to Platja Son Moll, lined by large hotels. Up on **Cap Capdepera** there's a lighthouse with fine views of the coast. If it's clear, you'll be able to see Menorca. The cape takes its name from nearby **Capdepera**, a storybook town with crenellated battlements of the 14th-century castle (Castell de Capdepera) on the hill above the town.

The agreeable country town of **Artà,** 8 km (5 miles) inland, seems far removed from the tourism that rules farther down the coast. Steps lead up Way of the Cross to the fortified church of **Santuari de Sant Salvador**, where you are rewarded with a fine view of the town, hills, and coast.

A sign pointing down a side road in the southern outskirts of Artà says simply "Talaiot," but it leads to one of Mallorca's most important Megalithic settlements, **Ses Paisses**.

Lively, unpretentious Cala Ratjada is true to the tone of Mallorca's east coast resort towns.

Some distance away on the coast, Artà has given its name to the limestone caves called **Coves d'Artà**. The Coves de Drac, further down the eastern coast, get more fanfare, but the less commercial Artà caves allow visitors to get closer and better appreciate the awesome formations that have been brewing for millennia. Colored lights and Bach's organ music point up the name given to the lowest level, "The Inferno." Jules Verne is said to have been inspired by a visit here to write *Journey to the Center of the Earth*.

Two groups of caves in the vicinity of **Porto Cristo** make a cool change from the beach — and attract an interminable procession of tour buses. The overcommercialized **Coves del Drac** (Caves of the Dragon), to the south of the port, contain almost 2 km (more than a mile) of huge chambers and spectacular formations, as well as the unquestionable highlight — a 177-m- (581-ft-) long underground lake named after Edouard-Alfred Martel, the French speleologist who explored

Dramatic colored lights accentuate natural formations in the limestone caves of Artà.

the caves in 1896. There's no denying the grandeur of the formations and their atmospheric lighting. The grand finale seems spectacular to some and completely unnecessary to others: The lights in the amphitheater dim and three rowboats decked out with Christmas lights paddle out to the middle of the lake, one with an organist and two violinists playing classical music. If you wish, after the concerto you can hop one of the boats yourself and go for a little spin across the water.

Cala d'Or came early to the resort business, and it has now evolved into a huge complex encompassing several individual coves and resorts, with all the facilities and watersports you could ask for. In contrast, nearby **Porto Petro** still looks like a traditional fishing village, though it, too, is not immune from the summertime tourist invasion.

Cala Mondragó is practically undeveloped (by the standards of coastal Mallorca), and may stay that way by order of the regional government, which has become alarmed by the specter of unchecked building along the coast. One of the gems that first attracted visitors to this part, **Cala Figuera** is still delightful, with neat green-and-white houses and unpretentious boats lining its Y-shaped inlet.

THE SOUTH

Until recently, few visitors knew (or wanted to know) anything of Mallorca's deep south. Many of the coastal resorts that do exist are mundane, while large sections of the shoreline are simply inhospitable. The long sandy beach and dunes of **Es Trenc**, the south's best beach, were left to the islanders to enjoy. The situation is changing somewhat, but it appears that major development won't be permitted.

Cap de Ses Salines, the island's southernmost point, takes its name from the local salt flats and ponds, where many bird-watchers gather in the spring to see the migrants on the way north from Africa. **Colònia de Sant Jordi** is lined with hotels and villas, but it seems a rather half-hearted attempt at a resort. The nearby harbor serves as the starting point for trips to **Cabrera**, a tiny island usually visible 17 km (10 miles) to the south. Visits are limited to parties of bird-watchers or zoologists and to excursion groups.

Great Fakes

Mallorcan pearls are famous, but they don't come from oysters. Majórica pearls are cultured — that is, exquisite fakes — and manufactured in **Manacor**, the island's largest town after Palma. The pearl-makers have enterprisingly set up shop on the highway, and you can tour their factories. In the century-old process, glass beads are coated with a lustrous glaze made of powdered fish-scales and resin. After this is baked on, it's hard to tell the result from a real pearl. And since they're so good, the faux pearls aren't *that* much cheaper than the real thing.

Some 5 km (3 miles) inland from **Cala Pi** is **Capocorp Vell**, the most remarkable of Mallorca's Megalithic settlements, situated 6 km (4 miles) from Cap Blanc on the road towards Llucmajor. From as early as 1200 B.C. massive stones were being cut and hauled into place to build a village. The five talaiots (three round towers, two square) may have been added later.

THE INTERIOR

The name given Mallorca's vast interior, **Es Pla** ("the plain"), may not sound promising. And in fact, it doesn't slow down the great majority of visitors who stampede across the middle of Mallorca in a mad dash to their assigned piece of coastline. Es Pla is lightly populated and little geared toward tourism. Still, there are lovely agricultural landscapes with ancient stone *fincas* (farmhouses), terraced olive groves, farmers who still plough with horses, leisurely back roads, and unassuming old towns. It's an area best covered by your own transportation, either automobile or bicycle.

Northeast of Palma is the attractive town of **Binissalem**, the epicenter of Mallorca's wine industry (which earned a *Denominación de Origen* — a quality designation similar to the French *Apellation d'Origine* — in 1991). The town features a number of attractive townhouses dating from the 17th and 18th centuries. Farther along the main road heading

The Menorquí dialect includes some words picked up from the British in the 18th century. The subjects, presumably important in relations between the occupiers and the locals, concentrate on carpentry, food, and drink. *Neversó*, for example, is the name of a kind of plum. It comes from a comment made by Sir Richard Kane, the first British governor: "I *never saw* such plums." You'll also see *púdins* (puddings, or custards) and *píquels* (pickles), among others.

Mallorca Highlights

(See also *Beach Highlights* on pages 82 and 85.)

Cathedral (La Seu) and Museum, *Palma.* Beautiful 14th-century Gothic building with Gaudí altar canopy and ancient manuscripts. (See page 24)

Palma's Old Quarter. In the old quarter around the cathedral, several fine buildings, including: Palau Real Almudaina (14th-century Royal Palace); Banys Arabs (10th-century Arab Baths); Basilica de Sant Francesc (13th-century church and cloisters); and several Renaissance mansions with lovely interior courtyards.

Coves d'Artà, *near Cala Ratjada.* Largest of Mallorca's caverns, less commercialized than the Drach caves.

Ferrocarril de Sóller, *Plaza d'Espanya, Palma.* Spectacular 1912 mountain railway from Palma to Sóller; open-top trams to the Port of Sóller. (See page 37)

Parc Natural de S'Albufera, *Alcúdia.* 800-hectare (2,000-acre) nature reserve and wetlands with important species of flora and birds. (See page 45)

Real Cartuja, *Valldemossa.* Royal Carthusian monastery lived in by Chopin and George Sand in 1838–1839. With traditional Mallorcan folk dancing and piano concerts. (See page 34)

Coastal Road C-710, *Andratx-Port de Pollença.* A twisting road that tiptoes along the steep cliffs of Mallorca's northwest coast, passing spectacular overlooks, terraced fields, sheltered coves, and picturesque medieval villages.

Sa Calobra. A white-knuckle, 12-km (7-mile) road with more twists and turns than a rollercoaster (even doubling under itself at one point) leads to a much-visited cove at the mouth of a canyon, Torrent de Pareis.

Formentor Peninsula. At the northeast tip of the island, this lunar landscape promontory plunges into the surf. Further along the adventurous is Formentor beach, the famous 1929 Hotel Formentor, and a lighthouse and cove at the very tip.

northeast is the unattractive industrial town of **Inca**, center of the leather industry. The best reason to visit is to shop at the factory outlets. Inca's Thursday market sprawls through the streets, and tour buses arrive in flotillas, even though the goods are much the same as in other markets on the island.

Just north of Inca is the tiny town of **Caimari**, worth a quick detour to take in the amazing hillside of terraced olive groves, neatly layered among ancient stones.

Sineu, practically at the center of the island, is probably the pick of inland towns. Built on the site King Jaume II chose to build a palace (which survives, now much altered, as a convent), Sineu has an elegant Gothic church, some attractive seigneurial homes, and a pleasant central plaza with some good restaurants. Wednesday is market day, when people come from all over Es Pla for fresh produce and livestock.

In **Felanitx**, the honey-colored church Sant Miquel dates in part from the 13th century. In the street adjacent is a stone tablet commemorating a tragedy: During an Easter procession in 1844, the collapse of a wall killed 414 people. Felanitx is the starting point for a bracing trip to **Castell de Santueri**, a ruined hilltop castle that was fortified by every ruler from Roman times to the 17th century. Take the exhilarating walk round the ramparts — there's nothing between you and a dizzying precipice. The views of the coast are superb, and on a rare clear day you'll see Menorca and Ibiza, too.

Queso de Mahón

Menorca's cheese-making traditions are ancient. A fifth-century pastoral letter from Bishop Severo makes mention of "caseum" (queso), a staple of the Menorcan diet. A document from 1360 states that the people of Menorca offered cheese to the kings Jaume I and Pedro II. Italian merchants began exporting Queso de Mahón in the 15th century.

On the next hill to the north — and unless you're a serious walker you'll have to go back through Felanitx to reach it — the **Puig de Sant Salvador** is the site of a hermitage and one of Mallorca's most important places of pilgrimage. In the church, look behind the altar at the Gothic statue of the Virgin Mary, backed by an alabaster panel of blond angels.

Suddenly rearing up out of the flat lands south of Algaida, the 542-m- (1,778-ft-) high **Puig de Randa** is crowned by a monastery founded in the 13th century by the Mallorcan sage Ramón Llull.

MENORCA

For many years, Menorca — one-fifth the area of Mallorca, with a tenth the population — was one of the best-kept secrets in the Mediterranean. While it still receives only about one visitor for every eight that Mallorca does, the secret's out of the bag. Occupied by the British in the 18th century, Menorca remains hugely popular with English package tourists, retirees, and vacation homeowners.

The capital and largest town, Maó (Mahón in Spanish), and the former capital Ciutadella are on opposite coasts. Resort development is restricted to a handful of

Menorca's delightful museum is just one of the island's many treasures.

coves and beaches on the southeast coast and the west coast. Like a fish's backbone, one main road only 44 km (26 miles) long links Menorca's two main cities with coves, resorts, and beaches — as well as a handful of tiny towns — on the north or south coasts connected to it by a web of mostly one-lane roads. Many coves and beaches can be reached only by foot. Menorca's many Talaiotic monuments are scattered across the island, though they're especially concentrated in the southeast.

☞ Maó

Maó is the business and administrative capital of Menorca, but it remains, above all, a port. "The best ports in the Mediterranean are June, July, August, and Maó," said the 16th-century Venetian admiral Andrea Doria, noting that beyond the summer sailing season, a fleet couldn't do better than shelter here. The 6-km- (4-mile-) long, deep-water natural harbor, guarded by forts at its mouth and shielded from the winds by surrounding hills, caught the eye of the British Royal Navy early in the 18th century. In 1708, during the War of the Spanish Succession, the British seized the island for its port, and kept possession until temporarily losing it to the French in 1756.

British occupation, on and off until 1802, left its mark. The English introduced gin, and Menorcan gin production has thrived ever since (see page 96). Parts of Maó's old town appear straight out of Georgian England. Whole streets, including **Costa de Sa Plaça (Hannover)**, resemble 18th-century Portsmouth or Plymouth.

The only way to enjoy Maó is by foot. The city is clustered on a cliff; near the center, a twisting roadway (Costa de Ses Voltes) and flights of broad ceremonial steps lead down to the quays and port. Maó's star sight is its beautiful port,

Postcard from paradise — the placid fishing village of Cala Fornells reveals Menorca at its unspoiled best.

and the enjoyable promenade and restaurants and pastel-colored houses that line it.

At the top level, follow your nose to **Plaça d'Espanya** and the **fish market**, where you'll see more varieties of octopus and squid than you knew existed. Adjacent are a produce market and stalls, housed in the vast cloisters (*Claustre del Carme*) of a former convent, selling *Abarcas* (Menorcan peasant shoes), jewelry, and Menorca's famous Mahón cheese. Made of cow's milk with a small percentage of sheep's milk, varieties range from the young and mild to a hard-skinned and almost crystalline, long-matured version rivaling the best Parmesan.

The chief landmark in this area, on Plaça de la Conquesta, is the church of **Santa María**, a large Gothic space under a vaulted roof. Rebuilt in the 18th century, it was equipped in 1810 with a Baroque, 3,000-pipe organ — still played during organ concerts every morning but Sunday. Just round the corner, the stately

Ajuntament (Town Hall) is graced by a clock presented by Sir Richard Kane (1713–1736), Menorca's first British governor.

Elegant Carrer Isabel II, a long string of mansions overlooking the harbor, leads to leads to the Baroque church **Església Sant Francesc** and the **Museu de Menorca**. The façade of Sant Francesc, completed in the 18th century, conceals a delightful Churrigueresque Chapel of the Immaculate Conception. The museum, the best on Menorca, excels in its prehistoric and classical artifacts, which depict the fascinating history of the island.

Between the museum and town hall, amid Maó's network of narrow streets, is the **Porto Sant Roc**, one of the original city gates.

The legacy of British gin can be seen — and tasted — at the **Xoriguer distillery**, west of the ferry port. Established in the 18th century, the distillery still operates, and you can

The Camí d'En Kane, the original road that stretched across Menorca, is lined with attractive old haciendas.

look through big windows at copper stills bubbling away, producing a hot, colorless spirit, which is poured over juniper berries to become gin. You can sample any number of liqueurs produced here, including *calent* (spiced with saffron and cinnamon) and *hierbas dulces*, a bright green liquid (and acquired taste) that restaurant owners may force upon you at meal's end.

Take a stroll along the quayside, past the foot of the main steps, along Moll de Levant — where most of Maó's best restaurants are located — and you'll turn the corner into **Cala Figuera** (called "English Cove" in the days of the British Navy) and the Club Marítim, where pleasure craft congregate near the ships' chandlers, shops, and restaurants that cater to them.

If you have time, take a **glass-bottomed cruise** from the port or Cala Figuera for the best views of Maó, the harbor islands, and the forts on the shore. High in the hills of the north side is an imposing pinkish-colored mansion, Sant Antoní. Part Georgian and part Spanish style, the mansion is better known as **Golden Farm**. The house is privately owned, so you'll have to admire it from a distance.

Sir Richard Kane, the first British Governor of Menorca, moved the capital from Ciutadella to Maó, and is remembered by the surviving section of **Camí d'En Kane**, the original road connecting Maó to Ciutadella. Governor Kane, who seems to have gotten on well with the Menorcans, loved the island and devoted himself to improving its agriculture, education, and roads. He taxed alcohol to provide the revenue for these efforts. Relations between the islanders and the British inevitably turned sour, though, when troops misbehaved, religious arguments erupted, and later governors busied themselves with lining their own pockets.

Looking out over the harbor mouth toward vast fortifications on the opposite side (still used as a military base), **Es Castell** (also called Villacarlos) appears even more English than Maó. There are some lively restaurants and bars along **Moll de Sant Fonts** at the waterfront, and the **Cala de Sant Fonts,** a boardwalk cleaved into the rock framing the harbor, makes for a delightful stroll.

Excursions from Maó: South and East

This palace on Plaça Alfons III is one of many colonial-era buildings in Ciutadella.

If you set out from Maó, the first of many Talaoitic monuments is found near the city limit, at **Trepucó** off the road south to Sant Lluís. The *talaiot* and *taula* at the site have been slightly damaged, not least when the French army fortified it and mounted guns to fire on the British in Fort San Felipe.

Sant Lluis, a little town of checkerboard streets and all-white, typically Menorcan houses, was built by the French army as their headquarters in the Seven Years' War (1756–1763).

The southeast, with its small sandy beaches, clear water, and proximity to Maó and its airport, was one of the first to be developed for tourism. At S'Algar and Cala d'Alcaufar, villas cluster near a rocky shore, and **Punta Prima** has a sandy but often unkempt beach.

Though there's little to distinguish many of these resorts, **Binibeca Vell** (also spelled Binibèquer Vell) is something different. *Vell* means "old," which in this case is a misnomer. Inspired by a traditional Menorcan fishing village, a local architect created this sun-splashed "toy-town" of brilliant white houses and dark wooden beams and shutters in 1972.

Just up the coast from Binebeca are some of the southeast's finest beaches and swimming waters. Literally right next door is an area known to locals as **Las Ollas** — the name means "frying pans," perhaps pertaining to the circular shape of this natural swimming hole carved by the sea. More likely, though, the sobriquet refers to the sound of the continually moving waters, sloshing against a beautiful rock basin like sauces bubbling in a pan. The "pools" are popular with nudist bathers.

The road makes detours inland on its way west to the resorts of Binidalí and fine protected coves **Cala de Biniparratx** and **Cala de Binidalí.** Both are small enough and sufficiently off the beaten path that you're unlikely to encounter large crowds. The former has a platform at the edge of the sea, which provides excellent views of the coast and back at the small cove. To get to Cala de Biniparratx, park your car in the small lot and walk along a beautiful path through a canyon and shrubs to a narrow cove. The beach is sheltered by steep cliffs that house ancient cave dwellings.

Farther west along the coast is another spate of massive development. **Cala en Porter** is one of the largest, oldest-established, and, in season, loudest holiday towns on Menorca. This villa town — called an *urbanització* — is resolutely British. If you're looking for a pint of bitters and an English football game, you'll have no trouble finding it. Steps lead down the hill through sprawling development to

☞ a rather nice, but crowded, sandy beach. Nearby is **Cova d'En Xoroi** a cave carved in the steep cliff that has been converted into a disco. You can dance the night away above a vertiginous drop to the crashing sea. For those who are curious but not nocturnal, the enterprising owner allows afternoon visits for a reduced cover charge.

☞ In contrast to Cala'En Porter, nearby **Cales Coves** is undeveloped. Although no buildings survive, there's evidence that it was a port in Roman times. Cales Coves is best known, however, for its amazing collection of caves — perhaps a hundred or more — burrowed out of the cliffs. You can see the openings of caves once used as necropolises

Mysterious Megaliths

Menorca is sometimes called "the island of wind and stone" — a distinction which, not surprisingly, has never been used as the tourist board's tag line. So much is constructed of stone that being on this tiny, windswept island can sometimes feel like you've wandered onto the set of the "Flintstones." Across the island, property is divided by neat walls of stacked dry-stone. (Not only is the stone useful in demarcating territory, but farmers had no other way to clear the land.) All those walls represent millennia of superhuman effort by a population that in ancient times can never have numbered more than a few thousand.

Both Mallorca and Menorca (but curiously, not Ibiza) are also littered with fine examples of the prehistoric Megalith cultures that inhabited the islands. Especially on Menorca, where more than 1,000 such monuments have been classified, you'll find remarkable towers called talaiots and burial chambers, or navetas, in the shape of upturned boats. The uniquely Menorcan taula, a massive T-shape made of two blocks of subtly carved stone, was their masterpiece. But its purpose remains enigmatic.

(burial chambers) in the Talaiotic period; today some of them provide shelter for dropouts and backpackers.

North Coast

Wild, rocky, and deeply indented, much of the north coast can't be reached by road at all. Immediately north of Maó is the **Cap de Favàrritx**, a barren cape with a lighthouse. Down the coast is the attractive beach at **Cala Presili** and, inland, **S'Albufera,** a wetlands nature reserve distinguished by a freshwater lake, migrant birds, and sand dunes. From the small resort of **Es Grau,** with

Torralba d'en Salort — one of many megalithic sites dotting the Menorcan landscape.

beaches and swimming waters popular with families, it's possible to hire a boat to go to the beaches of rocky **Illa d'En Colom** (Pigeon Island).

The twin coves of **Port d'Addaia** — now a holiday village and harbor — were the site of the last British invasion in 1798, by Scottish Highland troops who probably thought these rocky hillsides covered with purple heather were just like home. You can drive down to the sea at only a few places, and inevitably some of these have developed rapidly into sprawling resorts. **Na Macaret** was an old fishing village, and much of the new development seeks to imitate a traditional look, especially around the neat little square.

Arenal d'En Castell has a beautiful circular bay, almost enclosed and with a wide sandy beach.

Nearby **Son Parc,** near a big, flat sandy beach backed by dunes, is an artificial creation centered around a golf club, the only one of its kind on Menorca. For greater authenticity, head back to the Maó-Fornells road and onto **Fornells,** which remains a real fishing village. This low-key town, a good base for exploring the north coast, is lined by pretty houses and ballyhooed seafood restaurants along the waterfront. The inlet's sheltered coastline and shallow water make it ideal for sailing and windsurfing.

For geological extremes, take the rough and pothole-ridden track to the most northerly point on the island, **Cap de Cavallería**. It's passable by car, with a farm gate to open and

Ciutadella, with its sandstone buildings and cobblestone streets, oozes Spanish colonial charm.

close, and leads past the site of the ancient Carthaginian and Roman port of Sanitja. Walk along the sheer drop of the clifftop near the lighthouse for breathtaking views.

Back down the hellish road from the cape, and due west, is the isolated beach **Platja Binimella.** Menorcans favor the orange-tinged sand-and-pebble beach on weekends. But if it's beaches you're after, you cannot do better on Menorca (or just about anywhere) than **Cala Pregonda.** You can only get here by scrambling over the hills just west of Binimella. About 20 minutes later, having passed through a desert landscape, you will have discovered paradise: a spectacular sandy beach framed by a lush pine forest and stalagmite-like sea stacks rising out of impossibly transparent waters.

West from Maó: Taloitic Monuments and Inland Towns

From Maó, plenty of people blitz right across Menorca to Ciutadella — only 45 km (27 miles) and a direct shot, it takes less than an hour. The busy main road from Maó to Ciutadella at first runs parallel to the one built by order of the first British governor, the **Camí d'En Kane**. The scenic and well-paved old road passes a number of handsome *haciendas*. Beyond Alaior, the modern road is superimposed on the old route.

Near Maó, you can begin a tour of Menorca's mysterious 3,000-year-old megalithic sites. Just 3 km (2 miles) from Maó, a lavender sign to the left points down a lane to **Talatí de Dalt**. Hop the small wall and walk through groves to discover an elegantly slim taula with a fallen stone supporting the base — which has led some to speculate that it was formed this way for a reason. (In all likelihood, the piece merely fell). Next to the taula is a dark columned room and nearby burial caves. The settlement here dates to the end of the Bronze Age, around 1400 B.C.

Back on the main road, a little farther west, keep an eye on the fields on the north side. You're looking for **Rafal Rubí,** a site with two stone structures shaped like upturned boats, *navetas* (prehistoric burial chambers). These were collective ossuaries, used for secondary burials of bones. If you crawl through the low doorway of the better-restored naveta, you can appreciate the spacious interior, over 2 m (7 ft) high, with shelves at each end. The other *naveta* is more of a ruin, but worth seeing for the beautifully recessed stone door frame, evidently designed to take a stone or wooden door.

Finding Your Way: A Language Primer

With the resurgence of the islands' own dialects of Catalan, places and streets previously named in Castilian Spanish on signs and maps are now usually given in local forms. Both may be used interchangeably, causing visitors some confusion. *Ca'n,* which appears in many place names, originally meant "house of," and *Son,* "estate or farm." *Bini,* derived from Arabic, signified "son of" (i.e., family). *Cala* means "cove" and *platja,* "beach."

English	Mallorquí/Castilian	English	Mallorquí/Castilian
Avenue	*Avinguda/Avenida*	Market	*Mercat/Mercado*
Road	*Camí/Camino*	Palace	*Palau/Palacio*
Street	*Carrer/Calle*	Passage	*Passaig/Pasaje*
Castle	*Castell/Castillo*	Boulevard	*Passeig/Paseo*
Center	*Center/Centro*	Square	*Plaça/Plaza*
Cave	*Cove/Cueva*	Beach	*Platja/Playa*
Church	*Església/Iglesia*	Town	*Poble/Pueblo*

Road Signs

Ceda El Paso:	Yield

South of the road, and most easily accessible by the narrow lane from Alaior to Cala En Porter, is the fascinating Talaoitic complex **Torralba d'En Salort.** Torralba has perhaps the most beautiful taula of all — certain evidence that the ancients were masters of the art of stone construction. Recent excavations and radiocarbon dating put the taula's date at about 900 B.C. The "Hypostyle hall" has one of the few intact stone roofs supported by columns. This site is one of the only ones on the island to charge admission and keep set hours.

The town of **Alaior**, a mass of white houses clustered on a low hill, looks at a distance like an Arab or Andalusian village. The old section of town, at the top, is the most attractive quarter. Alaior is famous for its cheese-making industry; stop at either the Coinga or La Payesa factory for a sample of *queso de Mahón.* To the south of town, a long, sandy, gently sloping beach and sand dunes have brought obtrusive high-rise hotel and villa developments to the south coast at **Sant Jaume** and **Platja de Son Bou**. Besides waterslides and windsurfers, the outline of a fifth-century basilica discovered in 1951, is visible next to the beach at its eastern end.

A turnoff from the Alaior–Son Bou road, signposted to **Torre d'En Gaumés**, brings you to the second largest and most varied of Menorca's prehistoric settlements. Don't miss the hypostyle court, with its central supports and massive roof intact, or the water cisterns carved out in the soft sandstone rock.

Choose a clear day and head for **Es Mercadal**, halfway along the main east–west highway (9 km/5 miles from Alaior). Here, climb the twisting but well-contoured road to the top of **Monte El Toro**, Menorca's highest peak. It's only 357 m (1,171 ft) high, but provides excellent views of the entire island.

Menorca is steeped in prehistory. Here, Naveta d'Es Tudons, near Ciutadella.

A horseshoe-shaped cove with white sand and turquoise water sheltered by cliffs and green pine woods has made the stunningly beautiful **Cala Santa Galdana** one of Menorca's most popular holiday destinations. To escape the crowds, take the path from the parking lot opposite the Hotel Gavilanes (disregard the sign that says *Coto Privado de Caza* — private hunting grounds) and walk 20 minutes through the woods along a fairly well-defined path. You'll come to **Cala Mitjana,** a secluded but popular beach. If you try to drive here, you'll have to pay to travel the access road.

Ciutadella

Perhaps the most enchanting city of the Balearics, Ciutadella — with its sandstone buildings, churches, and cobblestone streets — preserves the flavor of a Spanish colonial island town. Until the early 18th century, Ciutadella ("little city") was the capital of Menorca. The British, on the island mainly for Maó's harbor, moved the capital in 1722. Ciutadella's beautiful but narrow and shallow inlet simply could not compete.

Plaça Alfons III, on the eastern edge of town, marks the spot where the road from Maó reached the old city gates. The gates are long gone, but the cafés around the square — including the atmospheric Es Molí in an ancient windmill — probably began by refreshing thirsty travelers. Locals flood the old town in early evening. Join them on their *paseo* and stroll along the main, pedestrian-only street that bisects the old part of the city. It takes various names, beginning as Carrer de Maó; at Sa Plaça Nova it becomes Carrer J. María Quadrado, one side of which — the lovely **Ses Voltes** — is completely arcaded in Moorish style and lined with shops and restaurants.

On Plaça de la Catedral is the stately Gothic **cathedral**, begun in the 13th century on the site of the old mosque. The bishop's palace adjoins the church. Ciutadella's tourist information office is just across the plaza from the cathedral. The pedestrian-only streets of the **Es Rodal** area just south of the cathedral are replete with wonderful stonework, the buildings' honey color glowing gold as the sun goes down. Look especially for the carved doorway of the 17th-century church **Església del Roser** down the side street carrer del Roser (across from the cathedral) and two 17th-century palaces, **Palau Martorell** and **Can Saura,** diagonally across from each other on carrer del Santissim. Nearby is the **Museu Diocesà,** housed in a former convent and cloisters on carrer Seminari. It displays archaeological and ecclesiastical finds.

The carrer Major del Born leads west from the cathedral to dignified **Plaça d'es Born**, the ceremonial square on the heights above the harbor. Formerly the Moors' parade ground, it is lined with imposing buildings, such as the former **Ajuntament** (now the police headquarters) and great 19th-century mansions (grand Palau Torresaura and Palau Salord). In the middle of the square, an obelisk commemorates a brave defense against some 15,000 besieging Turks in 1558. The town fell after nine days, and the survivors were carried off into slavery. Concerts are still held at the 19th-century **Teatre del Born** on the north side of the plaça.

From Plaça d'es Born, you can view the **port** below, a long curving inlet lined with fishing boats on one side and pleasure craft on the other. The port, the focus of Ciutadella's nightlife, teems with seafood restaurants and open-air bars.

Prehistory near Ciutadella

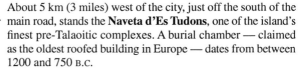

About 5 km (3 miles) west of the city, just off the south of the main road, stands the **Naveta d'Es Tudons**, one of the island's finest pre-Talaiotic complexes. A burial chamber — claimed as the oldest roofed building in Europe — dates from between 1200 and 750 B.C.

Two intriguing taula sites are hidden not far away. Heading away from Ciutadella, just after Naveta d'Es Tudons, take the next lane to the south, and after 2.5 km (1½ miles) turn left down a farm track to **Torre Trencada**. There is a signpost pointing across the fields to the taula and a huge cave. Back on the main road, take the next road turning south, through stone gateposts and across a farmyard, to the largely unexcavated **Torrellafuda**, obscured by trees. From the talaiot there's a wonderful view of the surrounding countryside, divided by rows and rows of stone walls.

Head out of Ciutadella on the road towards Sant Joan de Missa and branch off towards Son Saura; after 6 km (4 miles) you'll arrive at the prehistoric walled town of **Son Catlar**, situated in the farmland to the east of the road. You can walk round the 900-m- (2,880-ft-) long walls, which possibly date from about 600 B.C., though on the southeastern side you can see places where, much later, the Romans built bastions. The taula seems to have been deliberately broken off, and it is possible that the Romans used the precinct as a temple.

Beaches and Resorts near Ciutadella

Almost every accessible cove and inlet on the coast near Ciutadella has been developed in a rash of *urbanitzaciós*, creating a rash of holiday homes, hotels, and associated facilities. The resorts are easily accessible, but their sprawl is dull and suburban. Beaches here are very small, and over-crowded in high summer.

However, some of the island's finest beaches, near the middle of the southern coast, are probably best visited from Ciutadella. The sea is reached only by narrow lanes and farm tracks, but it's worth a trek to get away from the

A natural picture frame of cave rock...the town of Cala Morell shows signs of urbanization but all is not yet lost!

Essentials

Mallorca

Banys Àrabs *carrer de Can Serra, 7, Palma. Tel. 971/72 15 49.* Open daily April–Sept 9:30am–8pm, Oct–Mar, 10am–6pm.

Basilica Sant Francesc *Plaça Sant Francesc, Palma.* Open daily, 9:30am–12:30 pm and 3:30–6pm (note: closed Sun afternoons).

Cathedral Museum *carrer Palau Reial, 29, Palma. tel. 971/72 31 30.* Open Nov–Mar, Mon–Fri 10am–3pm, Sat 10am–2pm; April–Oct, Mon–Sat 10am–6pm; Sun 10am–5pm.

Castell Bellver *carrer Camila José Cela, Palma. Tel. 971/73 06 57.* Open Oct–Mar, Mon–Sat 9am–7:15pm, Sun 10am–5pm; April–Sept, Mon–Sat 8am–8:30pm, Sun 10am–7pm (July–August, Sun 10am–2pm and 4pm–9pm).

Museu de Mallorca *Portella, 5, Palma. tel. 971/71 75 40.* Open Mon–Sat, 10am–1pm and 4–6pm; Sun, 10am–2pm. Free admission Sat afternoon and Sun.

Palau Reial Almudaina *carrer Palau Reial, s/n, Palma. Tel. 971/72 71 45.* Open Oct–Mar, Mon–Fri 10am–2pm and 5–7pm, Sat 10am–2pm; April–Sept, Mon–Fri 10am–6:30pm, Sat 10am–2pm.

Poble Espanyol *carrer Poble Easpanyol, 39, Palma. tel. 971/73 70 75.* Open daily, Dec–Mar 9am–6pm, April–Nov 9am–8pm.

Real Cartuja *Valledemossa. Tel. 971/61 21 06.* Open Mar–Oct, Mon–Sat 9:30am–6pm, Sun 10am–1pm; Nov–Feb, Mon–Sat 9:30am–4:30pm, Sun 10am–1pm. Traditional Mallorcan folk dancing, Palace of King Sanç, Mon and Thur 11am–1:30pm; piano concerts every other day.

Son Marroig *Ctra. Valldemossa–Deià, km 65 (mile 40). Tel. 971/63 91 58.* Open Mon–Sat, 9:30am–2pm and 3–6pm.

La Granja *Esporles, km 14 (mile 9), tel. 971/61 00 32.* Open daily 10am–7pm (until 6pm in winter), Fiesta Mallorquín every Wednesday and Friday 3:30–5pm.

Ferrocarril de Sóller *Plaza d'Espanya, 2, Palma, tel. 971/75 20 51.* Trains run daily, 8am–7:45pm. The 10:40am tren turístico stops at an overlook, but is double the price.

Jardins d'Alfabia *Ctra. Palma–Sóller, km 14 (mile 9), tel. 971/61 31 23.* Open Sept–May, Mon–Fri 9:30am–5:30pm, Sat 9:30am–1pm; June–August, Mon–Fri 9:30am–6:30pm, Sat 9:30am–1pm.

Monasteri de Lluc *Lluc.* Tel. 971/51 70 25. Open daily 10am–5:30pm.

Coves del Drac *Porto Cristo, Tel. 971/82 07 53.* Open daily November–March 10:45am, 12pm, 2pm, and 3:30pm; April–October daily on the hour 10am–12pm and 2pm–5pm.

Coves de Artà *Cta. de las Cuevas, s/n, Capdepera. Tel. 971/84 12 93.* Visits every half hour, daily Jul–Sept, 10am–7pm; Oct–Jun, 10am–5pm.

Castell de Capdepera *Capdepera, tel. 971/81 87 46.* Open Nov–Mar, 10am–5pm; April–Oct, 10am–8pm.

S'Albufera *Alcúdia.* Tel. 971/89 22 50. Open daily, April–Sept 9am–7pm, Oct–Mar 9am–5pm.

Menorca

Museu de Menorca *Avda. del Doctor Guárdia, s/n, Maó. Tel. 971/35 09 55.* Open Tues–Sat, 10am–2pm and 5–8pm, Sun 10am–2pm.

Xoriguer distillery *quayside, Maó. Tel 971/36 21 97.* Open Mon–Fri 8am–7pm, Sat 9am–1pm.

Catedral de Ciutadella *Plaça de la Catedral, Ciutadella.* Open Mon–Sat 9am–1pm and 6–8pm.

Museu Diocesà *carrer del Seminari, Ciutadella. Tel. 971/3851 36.* Open May–Oct, Tues–Sun 10am–1:30pm. Winter hours vary.

crowds. The twin coves of **Macarella** and **Macarelleta** are stunning, with the kind of calm turquoise waters and spectacular sea views Menorca is known for. Macarella is perhaps the nicest fully serviced beach on Mallorca; the beautiful cove has an excellent bar-restaurant, open daily. Macarelleta, a nudist beach, is lovelier still. To get to it, take the path to the right of Macarella, a 10-minute walk along the cliff.

Occasionally there are times when so many head for the remote spots that they create a crowd there, too. A favorite spot for both locals and tourists is pretty **Cala en Turqueta**, 10 km (6 miles) from Ciutadella along the Sant Joan de Missa road.

West and south of Ciutadella are the busiest and dreariest of Menorca's resorts, including **Santandria, Cala Blanca, Cap d'Artrutx**, and **Cala en Bosç**. Just west of Ciutadella, **Cala Blanes** and the vast area of villas and hotels near **Cala Forcat** make a self-contained holiday town, though their two often scruffy little beaches can hardly cope with the summer influx.

The northwest corner of the island, in total contrast, is almost untouched by tourism, and environmentalists are winning supporters who want it declared off-limits for development. Some building at **Cala Morell** (8 km/5 miles northwest of Ciutadella) has jumped the gun, and a number of little white houses and blocks of villas have sprouted on the eastern side of one of the loveliest bays on the north coast. A maze of paths leads down to the rocky shore and around the cliffs — a geology textbook of tortured strata. Carved into the rock above the bay is a prehistoric necropolis dating from the 6th century B.C., including a cell with a sculpted façade. The oldest caves, though, are pre-Talaoitic, dating from around 1200 B.C. West of Cala Morell are the lovely, remote beaches of **Algaiarens**.

WHAT TO DO

SHOPPING

Though Spain may not be the bargain-basement destination it was in the 1960s and 1970s, it is still less expensive than most other European countries. You'll find a number of excellent deals in the Balearics, particularly on handcrafts, leather goods, glass, and ceramics. There are flea markets and weekly markets in many small towns (see box, page 77). On Saturday mornings in Palma, the crowds flock to the **Baratillo**, or flea market (even the signs on city buses call it by its English name). There you're sure to find everything from fans to fossils, and bargains include Mallorca's artificial pearls and lace — offered at "liquidation" prices by the sellers.

Best Buys

Mallorca and Menorca are justly famous for their **leather industries**. Since the 13th century, islanders have been making quality shoes, some of the finest leather and suede clothing, and exquisite handbags come from the islands. The focus of the leather industry in Mallorca are the factories in Inca; you can visit them and shop at the factory outlets (though prices will be lower than on mainland Spain or your home country, they may not be any cheaper than what you'll find in Palma). Menorca, Ciutadella, and Alaior are known for their leather goods. Of special interest among Menorcan footwear are **Abarcas,** flat, slipper-like sandals worn by peasants for centuries. In response to the tourism industry, they have grown progressively less simple—all kinds of colors and skins are now available—but you can still get the original, endearingly simple Abarca, in brown, navy, black, and yellow, for less than €20.

Mallorcan **cultured (artificial) pearls**, manufactured in Manacor (see page 49), are exported in great numbers. They're a good buy on the island, and prices do not vary much from shop to shop. There may be a small savings at the factory showrooms in Manacor, where you'll have the biggest choice.

Mallorca's **embroidered linens** for the table and bed are quite attractive. The fair of Llucmajor, the second Sunday in October, is a great place to find excellent examples. Other towns known for embroidery are Manacor, Pollença, and Artà. In Palma, the shops Can Bonet and Dana sell fine handmade embroidery. Woven cotton and linen are also a good buy. Look for the typically Mallorcan *teles de llengues* (painted fabrics, in green, blue, and pink, used for decoration in peasant houses). Handmade **baskets** are also a specialty. Renowned Mallorcan **glassware** has been manufactured on

Even just a simple produce store beckons you in...Mallorca has no shortage of money-spending opportunities to offer.

the island since the 14th century. The Gordiola factory, with a fascinating museum, is on the road to Manacor from Palma. Authentically Mallorcan are the **pottery** figures called *siurells,* painted in red and green on white on baked, whitewashed clay. Similar relics have been around since Phoenician times. They have a spout-like whistle, and rather phallic versions are grounded in fertility lore.

Wines and many other **alcoholic drinks** are still cheap by the standards of the rest of Europe. This applies especially to foreign brands made under license in Spain. Cuban **cigars** are significantly less than you would pay elsewhere in Western Europe, though legally they cannot be taken back to the US.

Shopping Tips

Palma overshadows all other towns on Mallorca in the scale and sophistication of its shops. Palma's excellent selection of chic shoe, bag, and clothing stores is concentrated along Avinguda del Rei Jaume III, Passeig d'es Born, and Conquistador. Look out for jewelry along carrer Plateria, and try carrer Jaume II for clothing and fans. Plaça Major holds a craft market every Friday and Saturday. On Menorca, both Mahón and Ciutadella have smaller but attractive pedestrian-only shopping areas.

Tax Back

For non-residents of the EU, the value-added tax (IVA) imposed on most goods can be refunded on major purchases. A minimum of €90. must be spent in a single shop. To obtain the rebate, simply fill in a form provided by the shop where you purchase the goods. One copy is kept by the shop; the others must be presented at customs on your departure, along with the goods. The rebate can either be credited to your credit card or forwarded to you at your home address.

Shopping Hours

Most stores are open from 9:00am to 1 or 1:30pm, closing midday for lunch and siesta, and again from 4:30 or 5 to 8pm. Big department stores and supermarkets of Palma buck tradition and remain open all day. In summer, shops in resort areas may stay open until 10pm. Almost all stores are closed on Sundays.

ENTERTAINMENT

Folklore and Festivals

Mallorcan cultured pearls are exported around the world, and are a very good buy.

With the revival of island dialects has come a renewed interest in Balearic culture. Children learn many traditional dances, and shows are put on by **folk dance** troupes at resorts as well as during fiestas. The oldest dances are survivors from Moorish times, and are usually performed in mountain villages. Dances are held in Algaida on 25 July and 16 August and in Montuiri on 24 July and 15, 23, and 24 August. The dance of *els cavallets* is performed in Pollença on 2 August at the Día de la Patrona, and in Felanitx on 20 July and again on the Día de Sant Augustí on 28 August. Another dance, the *parado*, resembles a courtly minuet: it is performed in Valldemossa in the square beside the monastery. The distinctive dances of Menorca include the *ball d'es cossil*, thought to be derived from Scottish dancing.

The dance, something like the English maypole dance, is performed during the fiesta in Es Migjorn Gran.

Late Island Nights

In Palma and the major tourist resorts, **discos** are a primary diversion for the beach crowd. They're not as frenetic, though, as on sister island Ibiza, where the mayhem is legendary. You may be offered tickets to buy while lying on the beach, or even free ones if the owners are trying to boost a place, or if the *tiquetero* thinks that your good looks will be an asset. There are **bars** of all kinds everywhere, some local, but more often than not with French, British, Scandinavian, and German décors, accents, and beers.

Large package **hotels** offer entertainers operating in two or three languages to loosen up the older crowd with competi-

---

Market Days

The same sellers often move with their goods from town to town, so markets don't vary much. All but the smallest places have one, on the same day each week and usually in the morning (as shown below, except where marked "pm").

Sunday Alcúdia, Felanitx, Inca (flea market), Lluchmajor, Muro, Sa Pobla, Pollença, Santa María.

Monday Calvià, Manacor, Es Castell.

Tuesday Alcúdia, Artà, Lluchmajor, Santa Margalida, Maó.

Wednesday Andratx, Capdepera, Colònia Sant Jordi, Port de Pollença, Sineu.

Thursday Alaior, Campos, Inca, S'Arenal, Ses Salines, Alaior.

Friday Alaró (pm), Algaida, Binissalem, Santa Eugenia, Son Servera, Ciutadella.

Saturday Bunyola, Cala Ratjada, Ciutadella, Palma (with flea market), Maó, Sóller (with flea market).

Where better to sip a cerveza or two than at a Mallorcan seaside bar? This one is actually carved out of an ancient cave.

tions, sing-alongs, and a more sedate sort of dancing. Hotels sometimes organize **flamenco** nights; even though these songs and dances come from Andalusia, they have become a feature of holidays throughout Spain. The shows are usually pretty touristy, concentrating on the more cheerful *cante chico* (light song) rather than the deep, emotional *cante jondo* (song of the soul). Still, the singers, dancers, guitarists, and flashy, colorful costumes are enjoyable to all but the purist.

For concerts, the **Auditorium** on Palma's waterfront has a regular schedule of events from opera to heavy metal. **Films** are usually screened dubbed into Spanish, with rare exceptions in the biggest resorts. Maó has a charming outdoor cinema festival, *Cinema a la Fresca,* near Parc des Freginal, during August and September.

Although Ibiza is best known for its **gay nightlife**, Mallorca, and to a lesser extent Menorca, also have a spate of nightlife options aimed at alternative lifestyles. In Palma, the best option is to contact the association Ben Amics (carrer Impremta, 1-1; Tel. 971/72 30 58) for a list of cafés, bars, discos, restaurants and hotels that are gay-friendly.

SPORTS

Although new leisure pursuits are drawing visitors to the Balearics, the primary aim of most summer visitors still revolves around sun and, most of all, water. Besides the beach, water sports, especially boating and sailing, are the islands' primary draw.

Swimming. Gently sloping expanses of sand, rocks to dive off into the deep waters of the Mediterranean, sheltered bay, or open sea: the choice is enormous, so try to find out what the beach is like before you choose your resort. For learning

---

Major Music Festivals

Summer festivals of classical music are held from July to September; further information can be obtained by calling the numbers given below.

Festival of Deià: San Marroig and parish church of Deià; Tel. 971/63 91 78.

Frédéric Chopin Festival: Real Cartuja de Valldemossa; Tel. 971/61 23 51.

Festival of Pollença: Cloister of Santo Domingo Convent; Tel. 971/53 06 69

Summer Music Festival of Ciutadella: Cloister of the seminary; Tel. 971/38 04 45

International Classical Music Festival: Santa Maria Church, Maó; Tel. 971/35 23 08 or 971/15 12 09.

Classical Music Nights, Fornells: Església de Sant Antoni; Tel. 971/37 66 11.

---

to windsurf (boardsail), choose somewhere with plenty of shallow water (such as Ses Salines on Menorca). Although lifeguards are rare, larger beaches do have first-aid stations. Just a few more words of warning: Beware of spiky sea urchins when swimming off rocks. Take along plenty of protective sunscreen — Factor 20 or 30.

Boating and sailing. The Balearics are a sailing paradise, with safe harbors and marinas a short cruise from quiet coves. Thousands keep their own boats here year-round. You can hire various sorts of craft for an hour, day, or week, at many beaches and hotels (but note that you will be required to produce a valid proof of qualification for a self-drive motor boat). The stately *pedalo* for two won't go fast, and it's stable enough for adults to take small children with them. For sailing lessons, the Escuela Nacional de Vela de Calanova (National Sailing School) offers intensive beginners' courses (Avda. Joan Miró, Cala Major; Tel. 971/40 25 12). There are also windsurfing

Windsurfing, water skiing, boating...name your watersport and Mallorca will provide.

(boardsailing) schools, and you can find boards to hire and conditions to suit everyone. Pick up the "Boat Excursions" leaflet put out by the Balearic Tourism Office for information about organized boating trips around both islands.

Snorkeling and diving. Take your mask and flippers — the water is crystal clear, especially off rocks and away from near-landlocked harbors. To spear-fish you need a license, and must be 200 m (650 ft) or more from the beach. Scuba-diving equipment is for hire, if you have a qualification from your home country. To obtain this diploma during your holiday, you can take a five-day series of lessons, usually starting in a hotel pool and graduating to supervised dives to a depth of 12 m (39 ft).

Fishing. Locals and visitors alike enjoy fishing from rocky shores and harbor jetties. Some experts say there's a greater chance of a making a catch in the cooler days of spring and autumn, and in the hours after sunset. To fish from a boat, obtain a license from the Commandancia de Marina, Moll Muelle Viejo s/n, Palma (Tel. 971/71 13 71), and for freshwater fishing in the reservoirs of Gorg Blau and Pla de Cúber, obtain a permit from SECONA, Passatge de Guillermo de Torrela, 1, Palma (Tel. 971/71 74 40).

Walking and Hiking. Mallorca in particular is perfect for dedicated hikers and novice walkers. Some of the hilltop castles and more remote stretches of coast can only be reached on foot. April and May, with a wild profusion of

---

Water Sports Central

Information on windsurfing, water skiing, sailing, diving, and the hiring of boats, can be had by contacting the Federación Balear de Vela (Balearic Sailing Club), Tel. 971/40 24 12.

---

flowers, are the best months. In the hotter months, start early or make use of the long evenings. On Mallorca the northwest mountains make for the most dramatic scenery, to be seen on the climb to Castell d'Alaró (see page 39) as well as between the Monastery of Lluc and the coast. On Menorca, search for more elusive prehistoric sites, or take the cliff paths of the

Mallorca: Beach Highlights

Cala Portals Vells: Three small coves set amid cliffs, pine trees, and caves, with fine sand, good road access, and a number of facilities, including a bar-restaurant and pedalboat hire. Cala El Mago is a nudist beach.

Cala de Deià: A beautiful rocky cove 2 km (about 1 mile) from the main road, with short walk to the beach. Restaurants and clear water. Crowded in high summer.

Cala Tuent: A well-kept secret off the twisting, over-crowded road to Sa Calobra — breathtaking scenery, pebbly beach, crystal-clear water, and good snorkeling.

Cala Sant Vicenç: Three small coves with fine sand and incredible turquoise, crystal-clear water, but a strong undertow when rough. Good road access and facilities, including bars, restaurants, hotels, and pedalboats.

Platja de Formentor: Beautiful beach looking across Pollença bay, with rocky inlets, fine sand, and pebbles. Easy road access and ferry from Port de Pollença. Excellent facilities: snack bars, pedalos, water-skiing, windsurfing.

Badía d'Alcúdia: The longest beach on the island is excellent for children, with 17 km (10½ miles) of fine sand. On the south side of the bay, Son Serra Marina and Colònia de San Pedro are quieter.

Platja des Trenc: Near Colònia de Sant Jordi, a long, wide beach with white sand, clear water, and dunes. Access by car via a track near Ses Salines. Several bars and other beach facilities.

Tee off in scenic splendor. Golf is a popular pastime on Mallorca and there are no shortage of attractive courses.

northwest or south coasts. The Balearic Government Tourist Office puts out a leaflet detailing 20 different walking excursions on Mallorca. Wear hiking boots or sturdy rubber-soled shoes for climbing over rocks.

Golf. There are 10 golf courses on Mallorca, three of which are 9-hole, the rest 18-hole. All are varied and challenging enough for the best players. You can also hire equipment and take lessons. Beautifully landscaped Son Vida Golf (Tel. 971/79 12 10) hosts the Balearics' Open, while the 10th hole at Golf Santa Ponça (Tel. 971/69 02 11), at 590 meters (1,966 feet), is one of Europe's longest. Tee off early: At times, you'll spend a lot of time waiting for players ahead of you. Menorca has a 9-hole course at Golf Son Parc (Tel. 971/73 97 58) on the north coast. For further information, contact the Federación Balear de Golf, Avinguda del Rei Jaume III, 17, Palma (Tel. 971/72 27 53).

Cycling. In the spring, thousands of serious cyclists come to Mallorca from all over Europe to race over the island and grind up the steepest mountain passes. Summer tourists make gentler progress on the bikes they've hired at the resorts. At any speed, a bike is a wonderful way to get around. If you're going to join in, check the brakes and tires and make sure a strong lock is included. Serious cyclists may want to contact the Club Ciclista Palma, on Gral. Ricardo Ortega (Tel. 971/46 75 71). Check out the "Cyclotourism Guide" put out by the Balearic Tourist Office; it details 10 rides on Mallorca and four in Menorca.

Bird-watching. The islands' resident birds would be enticing enough, but it's the visiting species that generate most excitement. Migrants from Africa stop to rest in the Balearics, and some stay for the summer. Birds of prey that are rare elsewhere in Europe are often spotted here, and stretches of water and wetlands, which include S'Albufera and Salines de Llevant on Mallorca, and S'Albufera on Menorca, attract waterfowl.

Horseback Riding. Ranches (*ranchos*) and stables are scattered over both islands, so you can hire a mount and go off

Mayo Days

It may seem like a strange distinction to have a sauce after your capital city, but the city of Maó is credited with the discovery — or at least popularization — of mayonnaise (mahonesa, from the Spanish name Mahón). It is said that the French commander Duc de Richeliu's cook came up with the recipe — spectacularly modest, of course: mostly eggs and olive oil — in the 18th century.

horseback riding. For more information, contact the **Club Escuela de Equitación de Mallorca** (Tel. 971/61 31 57).

Spectator sports

The Balearics are part of Spain, but **bullfights** are not the big deal they are on the mainland. They're staged on summer Sunday afternoons in Palma's large bullring (Plaça de Toros). There are occasional bullfights at the Plazas de Toros in Alcúdia, Felanitx, Inca, and Muro; Menorca has no bullfights. If you've never seen a *corrida*, be prepared to witness an ancient

---

Menorca: Beach Highlights

Cala Presili: Two remote beaches, Platja de Capifort and Platja d'En Tortuga, both with fine and rough sand, clear water, and good snorkeling. Road access is difficult: a track leads over rocks from the Cap de Favaritx. No facilities.

Cala Pregonda: Breathtaking scenery, sandy beaches, brilliant turquoise waters, and rocky islands in a protected area. Reached by a 20-minute walk along a path from Platja Binimel.la. No facilities.

Platges d'Algaiarens: A fine sandy beach, with crystal-clear water, in an area of outstanding natural beauty, La Vall. The beach is a short walk away from the car park (small fee required).

Cala En Turqueta–Cala Macarella - Macarelleta: A trio of popular coves, with fine sand and brilliant blue water, on the southwest coast. To get to smaller Macarelleta, a nudist beach, take the cliff path off to the right of Macarella. Beach bar facilities.

Calas de Binidalí-Biniparratx-Binissafúller: A mouthful of fine beaches on the southeast coast. Beautiful small coves with easy road access. Look out for the tiniest of beaches and "Las Ollas," a natural swimming pool with nude bathers, just west of Binibeca Vell.

---

ritual that for aficionados is more art than sport. Choose your seat carefully: *sol* means you'll be in the full heat and dazzle of the sun, at least at first. The more expensive *sombra* seats will land you in the shade, so *sol y sombra* means that you'll get some of each, though the sun won't be in your eyes.

Horse races are held every Sunday, all the year round, at the tracks (*Hipodròm*) at Son Pardo near Palma, and near Mahón and Ciutadella. The informal atmosphere and casual-looking handicap starts can be deceptive. The competition is fierce, involving foreign owners and horses. Betting is organized through a centralized "tote" system.

CHILDREN'S MALLORCA AND MENORCA

The Balearics' fine sandy beaches and sunny weather make them an ideal family destination. If the beach or pool begins to pall, kids can make a bigger splash on a giant waterslide. **Aquacity** at S'Arenal claims to be the biggest aquatic park in the world. The staff is safety-conscious, so parents can relax at the park's pools and cafés. The larger parks are quite expensive, so plan a long stay to get your money's worth. Other water parks are found in Magalluf, Alcúdia, and Sant Jaume on Menorca. More sedate is **Marineland**, west of Palma at Costa d'En Blanes, featuring dolphins, performing parrots, and sea lions.

Sling-along

The Balearic Islands were known during Roman times as the "Isles of Slingers," a reference to the sharpshooting locals who used to defend themselves against marauders with simple sling shots. The ancient defense is now practiced as sport. Visitors can check out sling-shot target practice by contacting the **Balearic Federation of Sling-Shooting** in Palma (carrer Olmos, 31; Tel. 971/72 62 50).

A boat **excursion** is an excellent diversion for both children and parents. Boats link all the resorts fringing the Bay of Palma, from S'Arenal to Portals Vells — if you wish, you can use them like a bus service. From Port de Pollença or Port d'Alcúdia, try a cruise around the dramatic cliffs of Cape Formentor. Sailings from Port de Sóller go to the rugged northwest coast, including the canyon at Torrent de Pareis/Sa Calobra. In the south, trips from Colònia de Sant Jordi/Campos dock at the strange little isle of Cabrera. A cruise around the historic harbor of Maó on Menorca is also fun.

You'll see rhinos, ostriches, and antelopes living happily in the **Reserva Africana**, a small safari park near Cala Millor on Mallorca's east coast. Visitors drive through as slowly as they like or ride on an open wagon.

Older children will appreciate **La Granja** near Esporles (see page 34). On this beautiful old country estate you can see craftspeople working and lively folk dance displays.

The charming antique **train** going between Palma and Sóller (see page 37) is bound to be popular with children of all ages. Mallorca's other line, from Palma to Inca, is not as picturesque, but it's a fun way of reaching Inca's Thursday market.

Whether in the water or exploring an old ruin, kids will have a ball on Menorca.

Calendar of Events

Saints' days, holidays, and fiestas are so frequent in Mallorca and Menorca that the chances are good that at least one will coincide with your stay. Banks and museums are closed on these days.

5/6 January: On the 5th, during the Procession of the Magi, the Three Kings arrive in all towns and villages. The 6th is Día de los Reyes, when children traditionally receive Christmas presents.

16/17 January: Sant Antoní, patron saint of animals. Bonfires, dancing, and singing during the evening of the 16th, best in Sa Pobla, Pollença, and Artà. Demons emerge in the afternoon.

20 January: Sant Sebastià, patron saint of Palma. A week of concerts, exhibitions, and events in the capital. The night before is revetla, with dancing and music in the Plaça Major.

February: Carnaval. Fancy dress and masked balls, culminating in sa Rua, a colorful procession through the streets of Palma on the Sunday before Lent.

March/April: Holy Week processions in most towns. Best in Pollença, Artà, Palma, Sineu, and Deià. The Davallament in Pollença is spectacular: the procession carrying Jesus on the cross descends the 365 steps of Via Crucis down to the parish church.

23-24 June: Sant Joan (St. John). A week of fiestas in Palma, Muro, Ciutadella, Sant Joan, Felanitx, and Deià.

29 June: Sant Pere, patron of fishermen. Sea processions, open-air dances, grilled fish, bread, and wine. Best in Colònia de San Pedro, Palma, Alcúdia, Sóller, Port de Pollença, and Andratx.

15-16 July: Virgen del Carme. Well-known sea festival; best in Porto Colom, Port de Sóller (at dusk), Mahón, and Fornells.

24-26 July: Sant Jaume (St. James). Street processions, open-air dancing, bullfights, and daytime events; best are in Alcúdia, Palma, Inca, Muro, Es Castell (Villacarlos), and devil-dances in Algaida.

2 August: Patrona de Pollença: Festival of Moors and Christians (Pollença). A week of celebrations, dancing, exhibitions, fireworks, and a craft show in the cloister of Santo Domingo. Mock battle between Moors and Christians through the streets.

31 December: Festa de Standa. Palma celebrates the liberation of the city from Moorish rule in 1229 with a Royal Standard procession through the streets.

EATING OUT

Along the resort areas on the Balearics, you could live entirely on fast food or Italian, German, or English cuisine served at beach cafés and resort restaurants. Many hotels seem to be convinced — probably from past experience — that a bland international diet is what visitors want. On some menus, the only indication that the Balearics are part of Spain is the listing of paella—though this saffron rice dish with permutations of seafood, onion, garlic, pork, rabbit, peppers, and peas is delicious, it's a traditional dish from Valencia, not the islands. Gazpacho, the cold and zesty "liquid salad" soup, and sangría are other Spanish imports from Andalusia.

Those hoping for something more — to experience the gastronomy of the place they're actually visiting — needn't fear; restaurants serving *cuina mallorquina* or *cuina menorquina* are readily available. The list of recommended restaurants on page 135 will give you a head start. Look for unpretentious places and half-hidden cellars.

Local Specialties

You'll find a wonderful variety of dishes to sample, with their roots in the different waves of influences that, from time to time, overtook the Balearics. Much of the best cooking is simple and robust peasant fare made from healthy ingredients.

Pa amb oli (literally bread with olive oil) has now evolved into a range of open sandwiches. At its most basic, country bread is spread with olive oil. Today's more opulent versions are loaded with cheese, excellent local ham, or *sobrasada* — a bright red pork-and-red-pepper-sausage spread.

Sopas Mallorquinas — in the plural form, as it is shown on menus — is closer to a stew than a soup, a combination of stewed vegetables, olives, and a little garlic, with slices of thick brown

As good as it gets...Outdoor café dining on the Passeig Marítim, Palma.

bread to soak up the juices. Fancier versions may include pork and mushrooms. They're all served in an earthenware platter, or *greixera de terra*, which in turn gave its name to a complete range of casseroles: *greixonera de peix*, a fish stew, and *greixonera d'alberginies* (or *berenjenas* in Castilian), a mouthwatering preparation of eggplant (aubergines).

Because of the easy availability of olive oil, it is only natural for islanders to sauté whatever is on hand. *Tumbet* is a ragatouille-like combination of peppers, eggplant, tomatoes, and potatoes cooked in oil. *Frit Mallorquí* is a tasty concoction of strips of fried liver, kidney, peppers, and leeks.

Peasant habits live on in Mallorca and Menorca. After a rain you'll still see people out at night carrying lights. They're looking for snails, or *caracoles*, which turn up on many menus, served with a garlic mayonnaise. Another once-abundant free supply of protein, rabbit (*conejo*), appears in traditional stews. Especially on Mallorca, every rural family kept pigs, and many still do. Pork and all its by-products are a mainstay, including hams and bacons, *botifarra* (a spicy sausage, either white or dark), and *lechona asada* (roast sucking pig), which is really a Christmas dish but featured year-round on many menus.

Mallorca's *sobrasada* — justly famous sausage made of pork and red peppers (the mild variety) — is something of an acquired taste. Try some: you may love it, and even eat it with honey, as locals do. The combining of sweet and savory flavors, and putting almonds in stews, surely dates from the time of the Moors. *Zarzuela de mariscos*, for example, contains shellfish, tomatoes, garlic, wine, and almonds. Look out for *panades de peix* (fish pies) and for seasonal savory pies — some are identified as the specialty of a single town; *espinagada,* which is an eel-and-spinach pie, is popular in Sa Pobla.

Crème caramel, or *flan*, is as universal on the Balearics as the mainland, but you ought to be able to find some sweet pastries and pies or some of the almond and honey desserts that are a delicious legacy of the Moors. Vegetarians should be aware, however, that even in confectionery, lard (*saim*) is an essential Mallorcan ingredient. It is the key element in the *ensaimada*, the light and airy pastry that's rolled up like a turban and sold in individual and family sizes.

Fish

It's not surprising that the islands are awash in an excellent array of fish and shellfish. However, the Mediterranean has been over-fished, and local fishermen can't keep up with demand, especially in summer. Additional supplies are either brought from Spain's Atlantic ports or frozen. *Salmonete* (red mullet) is caught locally. So are some of the *langostas*, spiny lobsters that are found on many a menu. *Caldereta de langosta* is a tasty lobster casserole, and is a big attraction in the fish restaurants of Fornells on the north coast of Menorca. *Merluza*, a Spanish standby, is hake, and *bacalao* is cod — frequently salted and dried, and not suited to everyone's taste. Farmed trout (*trucha*) and sole (*lenguado*) are imported into the islands frozen, and feature on many cheaper menus. Squid (*calamares*), cuttlefish (*sepia*), and octopus (*pulpo*) are also widely available.

Restaurants and Menus

When eating out, Spaniards generally eat a three-course meal at both lunch and dinner, including dessert and coffee. However, it's not uncommon to share a first course, or unheard of to order *un sólo plato* — just a main course — if you're not that hungry or looking to economize. Many restaurants offer a lunchtime *menú del día*, a daily set menu that's one of the best dining bargains in Spain. For a fixed price (often €10–15), you'll get three courses: appetizer, often soup or salad; main dish; and dessert (ice-cream, a piece of fruit or pastry), plus wine, beer, or bottled water, and bread. Typically, the cost is about half of what you'd expect to pay if you ordered from the regular menu. Most Spaniards will also order the *menú,* so there's no need to think you're ordering the "tourist special."

Reservations are only recommended at the most chic restaurants. Prices generally include service, but it's customary to leave a 5–10% tip.

Bars and Cafés

Bars and restaurants are an important institution in Spanish life. Some are open at first light to cater to early-morning workers; nearly all are open by 8:30am for breakfast. Open-air cafés are popular with tourists and locals all day long. One of the great pleasures of the Mediterranean is sitting

---

The Thing with Dishes and Prices

If you request the "menu," the waiter will probably think the fixed-price meal is what you mean. If you want to look at the full list of dishes available, ask for *la carta*.

When in Mallorca...Have a pastry and a café con leche in the Modernista bakery (Palma), and watch the world go by.

outside in the early morning with a *café con leche* (coffee with warm milk) and watching a town come to life. The price of a coffee also buys you a seat at a table for as long as you care to sit there. At many bars and cafés, you can get a selection of *tapas* (see box 95) and *bocadillos* (sandwiches) during most of the day.

Wines and spirits are served at all hours in bars and cafés. On the islands, bars are also called *cellers* (wine cellars) and *tabernas*. It's usually 10 to 15 per cent cheaper to take a drink at the bar rather than at a table.

Mealtimes

Beyond Palma, islanders eat a tad earlier than do people on the mainland. Breakfast may start at about 8am and go on until 10:00pm. Lunch runs typically from 1–3:30pm and dinner usually begins at around 8:30pm, although some people may be drifting in to eat as late as 10:30 or 11pm.

Tourists line the local pockets, though, so many restaurants make concessions to impatient travelers. Especially along the coasts, it's not a problem to sit down to lunch at 12:30pm or dinner as outrageously early as 7pm (the only Spaniards in the dining room at that hour, though, will be the help).

Breakfast

Except at hotels, which proffer mega-buffets as money makers or enticements, breakfast is a trivial affair in most of Spain, the islands included. (Check to see if breakfast is included in the room price at your hotel; if not, the hefty price may prompt you to try the nearest café or cafeteria.) In Mallorca and Menorca, locals may have a *café con leche* accompanied by *pan amb tomàquet* (bread rubbed with ripe tomatoes) or an *ensaimada* pastry. At the Palma airport, you'll see addicts taking home special flat boxes, nearly a yard across, containing *ensaimadas*.

Some bars and cafeterias serve not only great coffee but an "English breakfast" of bacon and eggs, too.

Drinks

Wonderful fresh fruit juices abound: Try some of the unusual thirst-quenching mixtures such as peach-and-grape. The local beer is fairly cheap, good, and served cold, but if you want the one you always have in the bar or pub at home, it's probably here, too. In the bigger resorts, there is a staggering—excuse the pun — selection of British, German, and Dutch beers, as well as other draught and bottled brands at about twice the domestic price.

The best Mallorcan wines come from Binissalem. You can also get a good selection of Spanish Rioja, Ribera del Duero, and Penedés reds and whites. Ordering the house wine (*vino de la casa*) is a useful economy measure — and many Spanish diners do it without a second thought. At better restaurants, it may be a pretty good bottle; at lesser establishments, it may be a wholly uninspired pitcher of table wine. Some restaurants will let you taste it, and if you don't like it, send it back.

Spanish sparkling wines from just outside Barcelona, called *cava,* are the world's best sellers. Some of these wines might be sweeter than you're used to; if you want it really dry, look for *brut* (even *seco,* "dry," may not be such).

Sangría is a favorite summer wine and fruit mixture — every bar has its own recipe. (Some bars, though, know it's an easy

---

Tasty Tapas

While the practice is still common in other parts of Spain, on the islands the days are sadly gone when you were given a free bite of food with your drink in a bar. You'll have to pay for the snacks to accompany your beer or wine, but the word for these morsels survives. *Tapa* means "lid," taken from the little plate that covered the glass and carried the snack. Some bars specialize in *tapas,* often featuring a long row of dishes, hot and cold, for you to pick from. Portions are larger now that you're paying for them: perhaps five different choices are enough to substitute for a conventional main course.

You don't need to know the tapa names—just point. It's a great way of making new discoveries among a range that might include meatballs, potato salad, tripe, eels, or stewed baby octopus. Be on the lookout for *boquerones,* white anchovies freshly prepared in vinegar, oil, and garlic, and, most common of all on tapa counters, the *tortilla española,* an omelette with potatoes and onions, fried in olive oil until golden.

If a tapa is too tiny, order a *ración,* a larger plate of the same.

Salud! Canellas is a tasty, locally produced liqueur made from dry herbs.

way to dupe tourists, and they use the cheapest wine, throw in a few paltry oranges, and jack up the price.)

To many, Spain means sherry (*jerez*), and you'll find every kind here. The pale, dry *fino* is sometimes drunk not only as an apéritif but also with soup and fish courses. Rich dark *oloroso* goes well after dinner. Spanish brandy varies from excellent to rough: You usually get what you pay for. Gin has been produced in Menorca since the British Navy was here (see page 54), and several brands come from the mainland, too. Other spirits are made under license in Spain, and are usually much cheaper than imported Scotch whisky, for example.

Finally, to round off a meal, try one of the locally made liqueurs, either aromatic *hierbas secas* ("dry herbs"), *hierbas dulces* ("sweet herbs"), or sticky *palo*, made from carob seeds.

Menu Reader

To Help You Order ...

A table for two, please.	Una mesa para dos, por favor.
I'd like a/some	Quiero un/una/algunos ...
menu	la carta

The check, please	La cuenta, por favor (El compte, por favor)

Tapas

aceitunas (olives)	olives
chorizo (xoriç)	cured sausage
croqueta	croquette (fish or chicken)
jamón serrano (pernil salat)	cured ham
morcilla	blood sausage
queso (formatge)	cheese
champiñones (xampinyons)	mushrooms fried in garlic
pan con tomate (pan amb and tomàquet)	bread rubbed with tomato olive oil
tortilla española (truita espanyola)	potato omelette

Preparations

al ajillo	in garlic
a la parilla/a la plancha	grilled
asado	roasted
salteado	sautéed
poco hecho/al punto/ muy hecho	rare/medium-rare/ well done

Fish and shellfish (*pescados/peix y mariscos/mariscs*)

almejas	clams	angulas	baby eels
atún (tonyina)	tuna	bonito	light tuna
bacalao (bacallá)	salt cod	boquerones (anxoves)	white anchovies
calamar (calamar)	squid	gamba (gambe)	shrimp
langosta (llagosta)	lobster	langostinos	prawns

The Daily Grind: El Café
café solo: espresso, served black
cortado (*tallat* in Catalan): espresso with a shot of milk or cream
café con leche: coffee with half milk (usually breakfast only)
café americano: coffee diluted with water.

lenguado	sole	lubina	sea bass
mejillón (musclo)	mussels	merluza (lluç)	hake
polpo (pop)	octopus	rape	monkfish
salmón	salmon	sardinas	sardines
sepia (sípia)	cuttlefish	trucha	trout

Poultry and Game (*aves y caza*)

codorniz	quail	perdiz	partridge
conejo	rabbit	pato	duck
pollo	chicken		

Meat (carne/carn)

cabrito	kid	callos	tripe
cerdo	pork	cochinillo	suckling pig
cordero	lamb	sesos	brains
ternera	beef		

Beverages (*bebidas*)

agua mineral	mineral water
agua sin gas	Still water
agua con gas	bubbly water
cerveza	beer
soda	refresco
juice (orange)	zumo
vino tinto/blanco/rosado	red/white/rosé wine
café sólo	coffee (espresso)
café cortado	espresso with a shot of milk
café con leche	coffee with milk
leche	milk
té	tea

Other

pan (pa)	bread	huevos (ous)	eggs
azúcar (sucre)	sugar	aceite (oli)	oil
sal	salt	helado (gelat)	ice cream
pimienta (pebre)	pepper	flan	custard
verdura (verdure)	vegetable	ajo (all)	garlic

HANDY TRAVEL TIPS

An A–Z Summary of Practical Information

A

ACCOMMODATION (See also CAMPING and the list of Recommended Hotels starting on page 126)

Prices are not government-controlled, but rates are required to be posted at reception desks and in rooms. Off-season, you may be able to negotiate lower rates, though many hotels in resort areas close for the winter. In season, many hotels are block booked by package tour operators.

Accommodation ranges across a broad spectrum. At the low end are rooms in a *pensión* (boarding house) and *hostal* (modest hotel); *hoteles* (hotels) are officially rated from one to five stars, with the top rating as "five star deluxe." *Hostales* are graded from one to three stars. Grades are more a reflection of facilities than quality: Some two-star places can be superior to others with four. The grading should be posted at the front door.

Small hotels in rural settings and former farmhouses, estates, and manor houses are considered *agroturisme* properties. They range from rustic to luxurious; many have pools, tennis courts, and minimum 4- or 7-day stays. Increasingly popular in the Balearics are package arrangements including accommodation in furnished apartments or villas. These are usually part of a complex with amenities, such as a swimming pool, gardens, or sports facilities. Finally, there is the option of staying in a monastery or shelter (*monasteries/ermitas/santuaris*). These are generally austere but very economical, popular with locals and outdoor enthusiasts.

Breakfast may or may not be included in the room rate; check before booking. A value-added tax (IVA) of 7% is added to virtually every purchase in the hotel, including the room, breakfast, phone calls, and minibar purchases. Telephone calls from your room, whether local or long distance, are extremely expensive.

I'd like a double/single room.	**Quisiera una habitación doble/sencilla.**
with/without bath/shower	**con/sin baño/ducha**

double bed	**cama matrimonial**
What's the rate per night?	**¿Cuál es el precio por noche?**
Is breakfast included in the room rate?	**¿Está incluído el desayuno?**
Where's an inexpensive hotel?	**¿Dónde hay un hotel económico?**

AIRPORTS *(aeropuerto/aeroport)*

Mallorca. Palma de Mallorca's massive Son Sant Joan Airport (PMI) (Tel. 971/78 90 00) has two terminals: Terminal A for scheduled flights and some charters, Terminal B for charter flights only. Taxis and regular buses link the airport with Palma, a 15-minute trip. Official taxi fares to all parts of the island are posted by the airport exit doors. The bus service operates to Plaça de Espanya (near Palma's two railway stations) every half-hour from early morning to midnight. Tour-company representatives and hotel coaches meet charter-flight passengers.

Menorca. Maó (Mahón) Airport (MAH) is 5 km (3 miles), a 20-minute taxi ride, from the city. There is no bus service. The airport's international traffic operates only from May to October, and many of its facilities (tourist information, duty-free shop) are open only during that period. Car-hire desks, café, and bar operate year-round.

Bus	**autobús**
Downtown, please	**al centro, por favor**
Tourist information	**informaciónes turísticas**
Map (city/island)	**plano (de la ciudad/isla)**

B

BICYCLE AND SCOOTER RENTAL *(bicicletas de alquiler)*

A practical and enjoyable way to see the islands is to rent a bicycle by the hour or day. Mopeds and motor scooters are also available in most resorts, but you'll need a special license exclusively for them. Prices vary widely, so shop around. Remember that wearing a helmet is compulsory when riding a motorcycle, whatever the engine. Ask the bike shop for a helmet, pump, and patch kit, lest you get stuck with a flat tire many miles from your hotel.

I'd like to rent a bicycle. **Quisiera alquilar una bicicleta.**

What's the charge per day/week? **¿Cuánto es por día/semana?**

BUDGETING FOR YOUR TRIP

The Balearic Islands are relatively inexpensive compared to other European holiday destinations. Charter flights and package deals can be especially economical.

Transportation to Mallorca and Menorca. For Europeans, the islands are a short, direct flight away. Regularly scheduled flights are expensive, but you are likely to find a wide choice of discounts and charter flights, especially outside of peak season (though even at the last minute, you may also find good deals during peak season). For those traveling from beyond Europe, the flight will be a considerably greater portion of your overall budget, though you may also be able to find packages and specials. You will likely have to travel through Madrid or Barcelona.

Accommodation. Hotels can be expensive relative to prices on the Spanish mainland (especially in the top categories). Yet so many island hotels operate on a tour operator basis that package deals can become extremely affordable. Aparthotels, rentals, and time-shares generally have more affordable weekly and monthly rates. See approximate prices in the following section, "Recommended Hotels."

Meals. Restaurant prices will be a pleasant surprise for most Americans, as even top-rated restaurants seem affordable compared to most European capitals. The Spanish institution, the *menú del día*, a pre-fixe midday meal, is an excellent bargain, often costing no more than €10–15 for a 3-course meal. Spanish wines are an excellent deal, even in fine restaurants.

Local transportation. The islands are small, and transportation is relatively inexpensive, especially if you use public transportation. Car rentals, though, can also be much less expensive than in other European countries (though higher than in most US cities). Taxis are affordable and a good way to get around within a city, but not recommended to travel from one region of an island to another. Inter-island ferries are affordable, though a flight may not be much more expensive (check for off-peak hours).

Incidentals. Your major expenses will be excursions, entertainment, and daytime sporting activities. Organized excursions are often quite affordable, but many of the purpose-built attractions (waterparks, safaris, etc.) are expensive, and tourist-oriented sights like caverns aren't cheap, either. Nightclub and disco covers are high, as are drinks once inside. Unless included in a deluxe package deal, you'll have to pay to play—whether golf, tennis, horseback riding, windsurfing, or water-skiing. All are affordable relative to other destinations, though they'll add up over the course of an active vacation.

C

CAMPING (*campings*)
Pitching your tent on beaches and parkland is illegal, and you'll be asked unceremoniously to move on. You may be able to camp on private land, but be sure to ask permission of the owner first.

There are two official camping sites on **Mallorca**, both at the north end of the island:

Club San Pedro, Artá (Cala dels Camps, Colonia de San Pedro), Tel. 971/58 90 23, open June to September. Situated 1.6 km (1 mile) from the beach with its own swimming pool, hot and cold showers, bar/restaurant, and supermarket.

Sun Club Picafort, Platja de Muro (Ctra. Artà-Pto. Alcúdia, km 23.400), Tel. 971/86 00 02, open all year. The site is within walking distance of the beach and has many facilities, including swimming pools, tennis courts, showers and baths, bars/restaurant, supermarket, and disco.

Menorca has two official camping sites:

S'Atalaia, Ferreríes (Ctra. Cala Galdana, km 4), Tel. 971/37 42 32, open all year. Situated amidst pine woods 4 km (2½ miles) from Ferreríes and 3 km (2 miles) from the beach (Cala Galdana). Facilities include swimming pool, showers, restaurant/bar, and supermarket.

Son Bou, Alaior (Ctra. de Sant Jaume, km 3.5), Tel. 971/37 26 05, open April to October. Situated 2½ km (1½ miles) from the beach. Many facilities include swimming pool, showers, restaurant/bar, and supermarket.

For the campsites listed above, you are advised to book ahead during the peak season in July and August.

May we camp here?	**¿Se puede acampar aquí?**
We have a tent.	**Tenemos una tienda de camping.**

CAR RENTAL/HIRE *(coches de alquiler)*

If you wish to travel a good deal around either island, renting a car is advisable. Most travelers covering Mallorca's north coast or explore quieter coves on Menorca rent cars. Major international— Avis, Hertz, Budget, National, Kemwell — and Spanish national rental companies — are located in both airports and in Palma and Menorca's main cities, as well as the major resorts. Many smaller agencies advertise 3-day and weekly specials (all with unlimited mileage). Some of these deals can be surprisingly affordable, sometimes as low as €30 per day. Rates are seasonal, and are usually much lower if contracted and paid for in advance in one's home country. Ask for special seasonal rates and discounts and find out what insurance is included.

A value-added tax (IVA) of 15% is added to the total charge, but will have been included if you have pre-paid the car hire before arrival (normally the way to obtain the lowest rates). Third-party insurance is required and included, but full collision coverage is advisable as well. Many credit cards automatically include this if you use the card to pay for the car, but be sure to verify this before departure.

Most sizes of car are available, including 4-wheel drives and convertibles, but the vast majority are small, standard-transmission, economy models. They're well suited to the narrow rural roads and mountain hairpin bends.

Renters must be 21 and have had a license at least 6 months. Rental companies will accept your home country national driver's license. Renting at an airport may incur a surcharge of up to €10.

I'd like to rent a car (tomorrow).	**Quisiera alquilar un coche (para mañana).**
for one day/a week	**por un día/una semana**
Please include full insurance.	**Haga el favor de incluir el seguro a todo riesgo.**
Unleaded gasoline	**petrol sin plomo**
Fill it up	**lleno, por favor**

CLIMATE

Sun-seekers hit the beaches from May to October, and the sea is pleasantly warm for swimming from June or July to October. July and August can be scorching as well as overcrowded. Mallorca enjoys a mild winter, too, offering a tempting break for visitors from northern Europe; more and more hotels are staying open in winter. It can be chilly and wet at times, of course, but a wall of mountains along the northwest coast protects the rest of the island from the worst of the winter weather. The tourist season has been getting longer: March and April bring a rush of cyclists, soon followed by walkers and bird-watchers.

Menorca can be swept by cold winds in winter and early spring. The holiday season here runs from early May to the end of October, with few hotels open the rest of the year.

Mallorca and Menorca

These average temperatures and sunshine figures apply to Palma.

	J	F	M	A	M	J	J	A	S	O	N	D
Max °F	57	59	62	66	71	79	84	84	80	73	64	59
Max °C	14	15	17	19	22	26	29	29	27	23	18	15

	J	F	M	A	M	J	J	A	S	O	N	D
Min °F	43	43	46	50	55	62	68	68	64	57	50	46
Min °C	6	6	8	10	13	17	20	20	18	14	10	8
Days of sunshine	15	14	16	19	20	22	28	26	20	16	14	14

CLOTHING

From June to September the days are always hot — wear lightweight cotton clothes — but take along a jacket or sweater for the evening. Remember also to take a long-sleeved shirt or sunhat to protect against the strong midday sun. During the rest of the year a light jacket and a raincoat or umbrella will come in handy.

Although the prevailing attitude is overwhelmingly towards casual dress, some restaurants and nightclubs object to men wearing shorts and t-shirts. A sport shirt and slacks should suffice.

Walking shoes and/or hiking boots are advisable if you are planning walking or treks during your stay. Take a small backpack to carry lightweight windbreakers and refreshment if you intend to tackle the hills.

CRIME AND SAFETY

Spain's crime rate has caught up with that of other European countries and the Balearics have not been immune—though they remain one of the safest places to travel to in Europe. Be on your guard against purse-snatchers and pickpockets near Palma cathedral and around the Plaça Major at night.

The rules are the ones you might follow almost anywhere. Don't leave valuables unattended or take them to the beach. Make use of hotel safe-boxes. Don't carry large sums of money or expensive jewelry. Lock cars and never leave cases, bags, cameras, etc., on view.

In Palma, report thefts and break-ins to the Policía Nacional, elsewhere to the Guardia Civil.

I want to report a theft.   **Quiero denunciar un robo.**

My handbag/ticket/wallet/ passport has been stolen.	**Me han robado el bolso/el billete/la cartera/el pasaporte.**
Help! Thief!	¡Socorro! ¡Ladrón!

CUSTOMS AND ENTRY REQUIREMENTS *(aduana) (*See also Embassies, and Consulates)

All citizens of the US, the UK, Canada, Australia, and New Zealand (adults and children) need is a valid passport to enter Spain (and stay for up to 90 days). For members of the streamlined European Union, the process is harmless: They won't even get their passport stamped (though they still need to carry it). Citizens of South Africa need a visa in order to visit Spain. Full information on passport and visa regulations is available from the Spanish Embassy in your country.

As Spain is part of the European Union (EU), free exchange of non-duty-free items for personal use is permitted between Spain and EU countries. However, duty-free items are still subject to restrictions. There are no limits on the amount of money, Spanish or foreign, that you may import. Departing, you should declare sums over the equivalent of €6,000.

I have nothing to declare.	**No tengo nada a declarar.**

D

DRIVING

Road Conditions. Main roads are well-surfaced, and Mallorca has a few stretches of highway, making it quick and easy to get from Palma to the east coast. Secondary roads on Mallorca are narrow but good; on the mountainous north coast, they have more hairpin turns than some drivers can handle. Menorca's main road between Maó and Ciutadella is very good, but can be crowded with tourists and trucks. Others can be very narrow, rough, and unmarked.

Rules and Regulations. The rules are the same as throughout Spain: Drive on the right, overtake (pass) on the left, yield to vehicles coming from the right (unless your road is marked as having priority). Front and rear seat belts are compulsory. Speed limits are 120 km/h (75 mph) on motorways, 100 km/h (62 mph) on broad main roads (two lanes each way), 90 km/h (56mph) on other main roads, 50 km/h (31 mph), or as marked, in densely populated areas. Spaniards routinely appear to disregard speed limits, but that doesn't mean you should.

The roads are patrolled by the Traffic Civil Guard (*Guardia Civil de Tráfico*) on motorcycles. Courteous and helpful, they are also tough on lawbreakers. Fines are payable on the spot. Beware of drinking and driving. The permitted blood-alcohol level is low and penalties are stiff.

Fuel Costs. Service stations are plentiful on Mallorca but not Menorca. *Petrol* (gasoline) comes in 95 (Euro super lead-free), 97 (super), and 98 (lead-free super plus) grades, but not all at every station. Diesel fuel is widely available.

Parking. Finding a place to park can be very difficult in towns — and not just in Palma. Most have "blue zones" (denoted by a blue "P") — metered areas where you must feed coins into a machine and leave the time permit on your dashboard.

If You Need Help. Garages are efficient, but repairs may take time in busy tourist areas. For emergencies, call Real Club Automóvil (Tel. 971/75 01 10 or Tel. 112).

Road signs. Most signs are the standard pictographs used throughout Europe. However, you may encounter the following written, in Spanish or amended into *Mallorquí* or *Menorquí*.

¡Alto!	Stop!
Aparcamiento	Parking
Autopista	Motorway
Ceda el paso	Give way (yield)
Cruce peligroso	Dangerous crossroads

Curva peligrosa	Dangerous bend
Despacio	Slow
Peligro	Danger
Prohibido adelantar	No overtaking (passing)
Prohibido aparcar	No parking

Car registration papers	**Permiso de circulación**
Are we on the right road for…?	**¿Es ésta la carretera hacia…?**
Full tank, please.	**Lléne el depósito, por favor.**
unleaded (fuel)	**sin plomo**
Can I park here?	**¿Se puede aparcar aquí?**
My car has broken down.	**Mi coche se ha estropeado.**
There's been an accident.	**Ha habido un accidente.**

Fluid measures

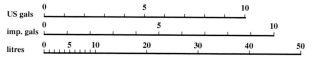

Distance

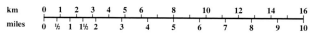

E

ELECTRICITY *(corriente eléctrica)*
220 volts is almost standard, but older installations of 125 volts, although becoming rare in tourist facilities, may still be found, sometimes alongside the 220-volt system. Check before plugging in. If the voltage is 125, American appliances will operate. If it is 220, you will need a transformer to operate them.

| What's the voltage? | **¿Cuál es el voltaje?** |
| an adaptor/a battery | **un adaptador/una pila** |

EMBASSIES AND CONSULATES *(embajada; consulado)*
Canada For minor matters contact the British consulate, Palma (or Honorary Vice-Consul, Menorca). Other cases: Consulate General, Edif. Goya, Calle Núñez de Balboa 35, 28001 Madrid; Tel. 91/431 43 00

Ireland (Honorary Consul): Sant Miquel 68 (8th floor), Palma; Tel. 971/71 92 44.

UK (also for Commonwealth citizens): Plaça Major 3-D, Palma; Tel. 971/71 24 45.

(Honorary Vice-Consul, Menorca): Carrer Torret 28, Sant Lluis; Tel. 971/36 64 39.

US (consular agency): Avda del Rei Jaume III 26, Palma; Tel. 971/72 50 51.

| Where's the British/American consulate? | **¿Dónde está el consulado británico/americano?** |

EMERGENCIES (See also EMBASSIES and, HEALTH & MEDICAL CARE , and POLICE)
If you are not staying in a hotel, telephone or visit the local Municipal Police or the Guardia Civil. Try to take a Spanish speaker with you. The general emergency number is 112. Here are a few important telephone numbers (check the front of the phone book for other numbers):

	Mallorca	Menorca
Police	091	091
First aid *(casas de socorro)*	72 21 79 (Palma)	36 12 21 (Maó)
Fire brigade *(bomberos)*	080 (Palma)	36 39 61 (Maó)

| Police! | **¡Policía!** |
| Help! | **¡Socorro!** |

Fire!	¡Fuego!
Stop!	¡Deténgase!

G

GAY AND LESBIAN TRAVELERS

The Balearics are among the most hospitable places in Spain for gay travelers. Mallorca in particular has a number of establishments, including hotels, bars, discos, and restaurants, that cater to gays or are gay-friendly. Many of beaches are also primarily gay. For detailed information, contact Ben Amics, the Gay and Lesbian Association of the Balearics, carrer Impremta, 1-1, Palma; Tel. 971/72 30 58; e-mail <benamics@oem.es>. In Menorca contact Ben Amics at carrer Arraval, 7-1; Maó, Tel. 971/71 56 70; e-mail <benamicsmenorca@altavista.net>.

GETTING THERE

Air Travel. (See also Airports) Palma de Mallorca's airport is linked by regularly scheduled daily non-stop flights from London and Frankfurt, with frequent flights from many other European cities. Regular flights from Dublin and Belfast go through Barcelona or Madrid. Flights from the US and Canada go through the same mainland cities. Travelers also have the option of securing the cheapest flight to Spain and then hopping an inexpensive shuttle flight to Palma or Máo. From Australia and New Zealand, the usual pattern is to go through London or another European capital, though regular one-stop flights may get you only as far as Barcelona or Madrid. Alternatively, once in London, it shouldn't be difficult to get a bargain fare directly to the Balearics.

From points in Spain, there are many regularly scheduled flights to Mallorca and Menorca from Madrid, Barcelona, Bilbao, Málaga, and Valencia, on Iberia, Air Europa, and Spanair.

In practice, many direct flights arrive daily, at both Palma and Máo, in season from several cities in both the UK and Germany, most of them charter flights. From the **UK** and **Ireland**, an enormous choice is available. Extraordinary bargains may be available if you can travel at very short notice, both for "flight only" tickets and for packages that include accommodation. For travelers from **North America,** most charter flights operate to Madrid or the Costa del Sol, and may be combined with Mallorca in a special package.

By Sea. Car ferries operate daily year-round from Barcelona and Valencia to Palma de Mallorca. The slower, overnight trip is 8 hours on Transmediterránea (Moll de Paraires, Estació Marítim, 2; 971/70 23 00); during peak holiday season, it also operates a faster ferry, which takes 4½ hours. Faster yet is private Buquebus (Moll de Paraires, Estació Marítim, 3; Tel. 971/40 45 20 in Palma, 93/481 73 60 in Barcelona; e-mail <reserves@buquebus.es>), which takes 3 hours. In high season, there are direct links to Maó.

Ferries between Menorca and Mallorca go between Ciutadella and Cala Ratjada (Cape Balear Cruceros; Tel. 971/56 33 36) or Ciutadella and Alcúdia (Iscomar Ferries; Tel. 902/11 91 28; e-mail <iscomarferrys@ral.es>). The first takes 75 minutes, the second closer to 3 hours.

HEALTH AND MEDICAL CARE

Standards of hygiene are generally high; the most common illness to befall travelers will be due to an excess of sun or alcohol. The water is safe to drink, but bottled water is always safest, and is available almost everywhere. Even most local people drink bottled water, *agua con gas* (carbonated) or *sin gas* (still). It is good, clean, and inexpensive.

There are doctors in all towns and their consulting hours are usually displayed. For less serious matters, first-aid personnel (called *practicantes*) make daily rounds of the larger resort hotels, and some hotels have a nurse on duty.

It is well worth taking out insurance to cover the risk of illness or accident when on holiday. This is normally available as part of a general travel insurance package.

Pharmacies (*farmácias*) are open during normal shopping hours, but there is at least one per town open all night, the *farmacia de guardia*. A list of the nearest after-hours pharmacies is posted in the windows of all pharmacies. Spanish pharmacists are highly trained and respected and generally speak a good bit of English; they can also prescribe as well as dispense drugs. In small towns, it may prove very difficult to find an after-hours pharmacy.

The health emergency number is **061**.

Major hospitals include:

Mallorca: Centro Médico, Passeig Marítim, 16 (Tel. 917/72 10 95); Creu Roja (Red Cross), Tel. 971/20 22 20.

Menorca: Hospital Verge del Toro; Barcelona, 3, Maó, Tel. 971/15 77 00 (open 24 hours for emergencies). Clínica Menorca, Canonge Moll, Ciutadella, Tel. 971/48 05 05 (open 24 hours for emergencies); Creu Roja (Red Cross), Tel. 971/36 11 80.

EU nationals with EU form E111 obtained well before departure can receive free emergency treatment at Social Security and Municipal hospitals in Spain. Privately billed hospital visits can be expensive.

Where's the nearest (all-night) pharmacy?	**¿Dónde está la farmacia (de guardia) más cercana?**
I need a doctor/dentist.	**Necesito un médico/dentista.**
fever/sunburn	**fiebre/quemadura del sol**
an upset stomach	**molestias del estómago**

HOLIDAYS (*fiestas*)

1 January	*Año Nuevo*	New Year's Day
6 January	*Epifanía*	Epiphany
20 January	*San Sebastián*	St. Sebastian's Day
1 May	*Día del Trabajo*	Labor Day
25 July	*Santiago Apóstol*	St. James's Day
15 August	*Asunción*	Assumption

Mallorca and Menorca

12 October	*Día de la Hispanidad* (Columbus Day)	Discovery of America Day
1 November	*Todos los Santos*	All Saints' Day
6 December	*Día de la Española*	Constitution Day
25 December	*Navidad*	Christmas Day
26 December	*La Fiesta Navidad*	Christmas Holiday

Movable dates:

Jueves Santo	Holy Thursday
Viernes Santo	Good Friday
Lunes de Pascua	Easter Monday
Corpus Christi	Corpus Christi
Inmaculada Concepción	Immaculate Conception (normally 8 December)

L

LANGUAGE

While Castilian Spanish is the national language, local dialects of Catalan — Mallorquí in Mallorca and *Menorquí* in Menorca — are widely spoken. Most islanders are bilingual (at a minimum). Many street signs appear in both Spanish and the island dialect, though sometimes they appear in only the latter. If you know some Spanish, go with that; though the effort to speak Catalan is appreciated, it is not necessary. English and German are widely understood in resort areas and by people used to dealing with visitors.

Everywhere you'll hear an all-purpose expression, *vale* (sometimes repeated three times or more—*vale, vale, vale*) meaning anything from "fine," "okay," "you're welcome" to "leave me alone."

The *Berlitz Spanish Phrase Book and Dictionary* covers most situations you're likely to encounter in your travels through the islands. The *Berlitz Spanish-English/English-Spanish Pocket Dictionary* contains a 12,500-word glossary of each language, and a menu-reader supplement.

Basic Phrases	**Mallorquí**	**Castilian**
Welcome	*Benvinguts*	*Bienvenido*
Good afternoon/evening	*Bona tarda*	*Buenas tardes*
Good night	*Bona nit*	*Buenas noches*
See you later	*Fins despr'es*	*Hasta luego*
Please	*Si us plau*	*Por favor*
Thank you	*Gràcies*	*Gracias*
You're welcome	*de res*	*de nada*
Hello	*Hola*	*Hola*
Goodbye	*Adéu*	*Adiós*
Do you speak English?	*¡Parla angles?*	*¡Habla inglés?*
I don't understand.	*No ho entenç*	*No entiendo.*
How much is it?	*¿Quant es?*	*¿Cuánto vale/es?*

Days of the Week

Sunday	diumenge	domingo
Monday	dilluns	lunes
Tuesday	dimarts	martes
Wednesday	dimecres	miércoles
Thursday	dijous	jueves
Friday	divendres	viernes
Saturday	dissabte	Sábado

Numbers

1	un(a)	uno (una)
2	dos (dues)	dos
3	tres	tres
4	quatre	cuatro
5	cinc	cinco
6	sis	seis

7	set	siete
8	vuit	ocho
9	nou	nueve
10	deu	diez
11	onze	once
12	dotze	doce
13	tretze	trece
14	catorze	catorce
15	quinze	quince
16	setze	dieciseis
17	disset	diecisiete
18	divuit	dieciocho
19	dinou	diecinueve
20	vint	veinte
30	trenta	treinta
40	quaranta	cuarenta
50	cinquanta	cincuenta
60	seixanta	sesenta
70	setanta	setenta
80	vuitanta	ochenta
90	novanta	noventa
100	cent	cien(to)
500	cinc-cents	quinientos
1000	mil	mil

M

MAPS

The maps of the islands and cities put out by the local tourism board and available at all tourist information offices are sufficient, even for those traversing the islands by car. Even though some roads are not labeled by number or name on the map, they are easy to identify and all roads are clearly indicated.

Do you have a map (of the city/island)?	**¿Tiene un plano (de la ciudad/isla)?**

MEDIA (*periódico*; *revista*).

In main tourist areas most European, including British and German, newspapers are sold on the day of publication. So are the Paris-based *International Herald Tribune* and the European edition of *The Wall Street Journal. USA Today* is also widely available, as are principal European and American magazines.

Most hotels and bars have television, usually tuned to sports (international or local), and broadcasting in Castilian, Catalan (from Barcelona), and *Mallorquí* or *Menorquí*. Satellite dishes are sprouting, and most tourist hotels offer multiple channels (German, French, Sky, BBC, CNN, etc.). Reception of Britain's BBC World Service radio is usually good to excellent. A good set will receive the BBC long-wave and even medium-wave domestic programs. The local radio station in Palma broadcasts in English 24 hours a day on 103.2 FM.

Have you any English-language newspapers/magazines?	**¿Tienen periódicos/revistas en inglés?**
Where's a kiosk?	**¿Dónde hay un kiosco?**

MONEY

Currency. Spain's monetary unit is the *Euro* (abbreviated €), which is divided into 100 *cents*. Banknotes are available in denominations of 500, 200, 100, 50, 20, 10 and 5 Euros. There are coins for 2 and 1 Euro, and for 50, 20, 10, 5, 2 and 1 cent.

Currency exchange. Banks are the best place to exchange currency, offering the best rates with no commission. Many travel agencies and *casas de cambio* (displaying a *cambio* sign) will also exchange foreign currency into pesetas and stay open outside banking hours. However, be wary of those advertising "no commission." (Their rates are much lower, so you are in effect paying a hefty commission.) Both banks and exchange offices pay slightly more for traveler's checks than for cash. Always take your passport when you go to change money.

Credit cards. Major international cards are widely recognized, though smaller businesses tend to prefer cash. Cards linked to Visa/Eurocard/MasterCard are most generally accepted. They are also useful for obtaining cash advances from banks. A credit card will usually give you the highest exchange rate, translated at the time of billing rather than the moment of transaction.

ATMs. Cash machines are now ubiquitous in Spain, but on the islands you'll find them only in cities and tourist resorts. They dispense currency in various euro denominations. Using an ATM with your credit/debit card is by far the most convenient and also the cheapest way of obtaining euros.

Traveler's Checks. Hotels, shops, restaurants, and travel agencies all cash traveler's checks, and so do banks, where you're likely to get a better rate (you will need your passport for identification). Try to cash small amounts at a time, keeping some of your holiday funds in checks, in the hotel safe.

Where's the nearest bank/ currency exchange office?	**¿Dónde está el banco/la casa de cambio más cercana?**
I want to change some pounds/dollars.	**Quiero cambiar libras/dólares.**
Do you accept traveler's checks?	**¿Aceptan checks de viaje?**
Can I pay with a credit card?	**¿Se puede pagar con tarjeta?**
How much is that?	**¿Cuánto es/vale?**

O

OPEN HOURS

Schedules still revolve around the siesta, and most shops and offices therefore open from 9am to 1 or 2pm and again from 4 or 5pm until 8pm or later. Many museums and other tourist attractions maintain the same schedule. Large supermarkets and department stores frequently stay open throughout the day.

Post offices are usually Monday to Friday 9am–2pm, Saturday 9am–1pm. **Banks** generally open Monday–Friday 8:30/9am–2:30pm (1:30pm in summer), Saturdays 9am–1pm (except summer). Hours vary from town to town. Some banks stay open until 4:30pm (Monday–Thursday, mid-September to mid-June).

Restaurants serve lunch from 1–3:30pm. In the evenings their timing depends on the kind of customers they expect. Locals usually eat between 8:30 and 11pm (somewhat earlier than on the mainland). Places catering to foreigners may function from 7pm on, and many stay open throughout the day.

P

POLICE (policía)

Spanish municipal and national police are efficient, strict, and courteous — and generally very responsive to issues involving foreign tourists. In both Mallorca and Menorca, dial **092** for municipal police and **091** for national police. The general emergency number is **112**. The municipal police station in Palma is located at Ruíz de Alda, 8.

Where's the nearest police station?	¿**Dónde está la comisaría más cercana?**

POST OFFICES (correos/correus)

Post Offices — all identified by yellow-and-white signs with a crown and the words "Correos y Telégrafos" — in Spain are for mail and telegrams; you can't usually telephone from them. The postal system has greatly improved in recent years and is now generally pretty reliable. Opening hours are usually 9am–2pm Monday to Friday, 9am–1pm Saturday. The main post office in Palma is located at carrer Constitució, 5 (tel 971/72 18 67) and is open daily 9am–9pm; the main post office in Maó is on carrer Bon Aire (Tel. 971/36 38 92); in Ciutadella, it's found on Plaça des Born (Tel. 971/38 00 81).

Where is the Post Office?	**¿Dónde está el Correos?**
A stamp for this letter/ postcard please.	**Por favor, un sello para esta carta/tarjeta postal.**
I'd like to send this letter.	**Me gustaría enviar esta carta.**
airmail	**vía aérea**
express (special delivery)	**urgente**
registered	**certificado**
How long will it take to arrive?	**¿Cuánto tarda en llegar?**

PUBLIC TRANSPORTATION

Mallorca has a reliable and comprehensive public transport system serving almost all towns and villages. Obtain an up-to-date bus and train (FEVE) timetable from the tourist information office). Note that that public services end early, at around 8:45pm.

Bus (*autobús*). Mallorca is well served by bus lines, and its buses are economical, clean, and easy to use. The drivers are friendly and helpful. Destinations are marked on the front of the bus, and each town has its own main bus stop or terminal. In Palma, most services start from Plaça de Espanya, Plaça Sant Antoni, or Plaça de la Reina. A Palma bus schedule (EMT, or Empresa Municipal de Transports) detailing all city routes can be had from the tourist information office.

Menorca's bus system is much more limited, but services run between the main towns. In Maó most start from Plaça Esplanada or nearby Avinguda J M Quadrado.

Taxi. Taxis in Spain compare very favorably with those in other countries. They're the best way to get around Palma, especially in the evening. Check the fare before you get in: Rates are fixed and are displayed in several languages on the window. If you take a long trip you may be charged a two-way fare whether you return or not.

Train (*tren*). Mallorca has two narrow-gauge lines, starting from neighboring stations on Plaça de Espanya, Palma. One goes to Inca, but the more picturesque line, which dates from 1912, links Palma and Sóller. It makes five runs in each direction every day (six on Sundays). The tren turístico at 10:40am makes an extra stop at an overlook (See pages 37–38).

When's the next bus/ train to…?	**¿Cuándo sale el próximo autobús/tren para…?**
bus station	**estación de autobuses**
A ticket to…	**Un billete para…**
single (one-way)	**ida**
return (round-trip)	**ida y vuelta**
What's the fare to…?	**¿Cuánto es la tarifa a …?**

R

RELIGION
The national religion of Spain is Roman Catholicism. In the city itself and the area around Palma, there are churches of most major faiths; the tourist information offices have a brochure listing religious services, including those in foreign languages.

T

TELEPHONE (*teléfono*).
Spain's country code is **34**. The local area code—in the case of both Mallorca and Menorca, **971**—must be dialed before all phone numbers, even for local calls.

Mallorca and Menorca

The telephone office is independent of the post office and is identified by a blue and white sign. You can make direct-dial local and international calls from public telephone booths (*cabinas*) in the street. Most operate both with coins and cards; international telephone credit cards can also be used. Instructions for use are given in several languages in the booths, which are widely distributed throughout the islands. You can also make calls at public telephone offices called *locutorios*. These are much quieter than making a call on the street, and a clerk will place the call for you. You pay for the call afterwards.

Local, national, and international calls can also be made from hotels, but almost always with an exorbitant surcharge.

For most calls, including international calls, at pay phones, it's wise to use a phone card (*tarjeta telefónica*), which can be purchased at any *estanco* (tobacconist shop; look for the sign "Tabacos" or "Tabacs"). To call, pick up the receiver, insert card or coin, wait for the dial tone, and dial. To make an international call, dial **00** for an international line + country code + phone number. Calls are cheaper after 10pm weekdays, after 2pm on Saturday, and all day Sunday.

If you wish to send a fax, you may do so from most hotels, though the charge can be as high as €5 per page. Fax machines for public use can be found in communication centers in most holiday resorts. E-mail and internet is also widely available.

Can you get me this number in…?	**¿Puede comunicarme con este número en…?**

TIME ZONES

The Balearics keep the same time as mainland Spain, and Spain is one hour ahead of GMT. Spain is generally one hour ahead of London, the same as Paris, and 6 hours ahead of New York. The chart below shows the difference between Spain and some selected cities.

Los Angeles	Chicago	New York	London	**Mallorca**
3am	5am	6am	11am	**noon**

What time is it?   **¿Qué hora es?**

TIPPING

Since a service charge is normally included in hotel and restaurant bills, tipping is not obligatory. However, it's normal to leave a small coin (about 5% of the bill) after service at a bar counter, and 5-10% on restaurant bills. Taxi drivers do not need to be tipped unless one gives you special service. Additional guidelines:

Hotel porter, per bag	€1.
Lavatory attendant	€0.30
Tour guide	10%

TOILETS

There are many expressions for "toilets" in Spanish: *aseos, servicios, lavabo, WC,* and *bater.* The first three are the most common. Toilet doors have a "C" for *Caballeros* (gentlemen), an "S" for *Señoras* (ladies), or a pictograph. Public toilets exist in some large towns, and most bars and restaurants will allow you to use their facilities.

Where are the toilets?   **¿Dónde están los servicios?**

TOURIST INFORMATION *(oficinas de información turística)*
Spanish National Tourist Offices are maintained in many countries:

Australia: International House, Suite 44, 104 Bathurst St, P.O. Box A-675, 2000 Sydney NSW; Tel. (02) 264 79 66

Canada: 62 Bloor St. West, Suite 3402, Toronto, Ontario M4W 3E2; Tel. (1416) 961-3131

UK: 22-23 Manchester Square, London W1M 5AP; Tel. (020) 7486 8077

US: Water Tower Place, Suite 915 East, 845 North Michigan Ave, Chicago, IL 60611; Tel. (312) 944-0216/642-1992
8383 Wilshire Blvd, Suite 960, 90211 Beverly Hills, CA 90211; Tel. (213) 658-7188

666 5th Ave, 35th floor, New York, NY 10103; Tel.
(212) 265-8822

1221 Brickell Ave., Ste. 1850, Miami, FL 33131; Tel.
(305) 358-1992

Major resorts on Mallorca have tourist information offices:

Palma: Plaça de la Reina, 2; Tel. 971/71 22 16. Santo Domingo,
11; Tel. 971/72 40 90. Aeroport Son Sant Joan; Tel.
971/78 95 56.

Menorca: Plaça Esplanada, Maó; Tel. 971/36 37 90. Aeroport
de Maó; Tel. 971/15 71 15. Plaça de la Catedral, 5,
Ciutadella; Tel. 971/38 26 93.

In Mallorca, there are also offices in Alcúdia; Cala d'Or; Cala Millor;
Cala Ratjada; Cala Sant Vicenç; Magaluf; Peguera; Platja de Muro;
Port de Pollença; Port de Sóller; Portocolom; Portocristo; s'Arenal;
S'Illot; Santa Ponça; Sóller; Valldemossa; and Platja de Palma.

Where is the tourist office?   **¿Dónde está la oficina de turismo?**

WEB SITES

The Internet is a good place to get information before you go. There
are several Balearic sites you may wish to surf, including:

<www.caib.es>   Govern Balear, the official Balearic
                    government site

<www.menorca.net> Tot Menorca, cultural and tourism information

<www.fehm.es>   Hotel Federation of Mallorca

<www.inm.es/wwb>   Spanish Meterological Institute, weather
                    information for all Spain

WEIGHTS AND MEASURES

Spain is on the metric system. For fluid and distance measures, see
page 109.

Length

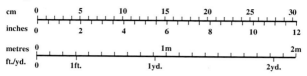

Weight

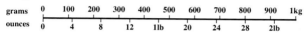

Temperature

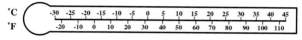

YOUTH HOSTELS *(albergues juveniles)*

There are two youth hostels, both in Mallorca, and they may be fully booked by school groups in summer, so you should reserve far in advance; as an alternative, try any of the monasteries listed in the Recommended Hotels section:

Alberg Juvenil d'Alcúdia, La Victoria, Alcúdia; Tel./fax 971/54 53 95. Overlooks Bay of Pollença; access by bus to Alcúdia, then taxi or 8- km (5-mile) country walk; 120 beds in 3-, 6- and 10-bedded rooms, each with shower and WC; facilities include dining hall, kitchen, terrace, TV lounge, and sports area. Closed November–March.

Alberg Platja de Palma, c/ Costa Brava 17, Ca'n Pastilla; Tel./fax 971/26 08 92. Close to Palma and the seafront area; 65 beds in 2-, 3-, and 6-bedded rooms, each with shower and WC; other facilities include dining hall, TV lounge, terraces, and meeting hall. Open all year.

Recommended Hotels

The Balearics were formally a maze of down-market concrete block hotels brutally clustered right on top of once-pristine beaches and coves. Today the trend is toward providing more discerning travelers with more authentic and upscale accommodations, frequently in old farm-houses and manor houses, as well as short- and long-term rentals. Many hotels on both islands are still beholden to the large tour operators. Only a couple of the establishments recommended below host tour groups; we make no effort to review the block-booked resort hotels, most of which are resoundingly similar in service, amenities, and facilities.

You are advised to book hotels well in advance, particularly if planning to visit between June and September. Regardless of when you go, it's not wise to descend on either island without reservations intact. Many hotels close for winter (December-March). As a basic guide to room prices, we have used the following symbols (for a double room with bath/shower in high season; prices do not include the 7% VAT, or IVA, tax):

€	below 50 euros.
€€	50–100 euros.
€€€	100–150 euros.
€€€€	above 150 euros.

Spain's country code is 34; the area code for the Balearics is 971.

MALLORCA

Palma

Hotel Born €€ *carrer Sant Jaume, 3; Tel. 971/71 29 42; fax 971/71 86 18; e-mail <h.born@biTel.es>* In a restored 16th-century palace on a quiet alleyway, this small hotel is one of Palma's best bargains. With a grand central staircase and beautiful courtyard under Romanesque arches, it overflows with atmosphere. Far nicer than its "two-star residence" rating. Reserve far in advance, even in winter. 29 rooms. Major credit cards.

Hotel Palacio Ca Sa Galesa €€€€ *Miramar, 8; Tel. 971/71 54 00; fax 971/72 15 79; e-mail <reserves@fehol.es>.* Housed in a grand and meticulously restored 17th-century palace, this tiny hotel — the only one in Palma's old quarter — feels like a luxury bed & breakfast. With antiques, terrace views, Roman-style indoor pool, Jacuzzi, and sauna, the Galesa means to spoil its patrons — and of course, that doesn't come cheap. Wheelchair access. 12 rooms. Major credit cards.

San Lorenzo €€€ *San Lorenzo, 14; Tel. 971/72 82 00. Fax 971/71 19 01; web site <www.fehm.es/pmi/sanlorenzo>.* A 17th-century house in a lively section of downtown, this charming *hotelito* is perennially booked. An excellent value with just 6 unique rooms. Rooms have balconies, garden access, or chimneys, and terraces (suites). Book very early. 6 rooms. Major credit cards.

Hotel Almudaina €€ *Avinguda Jaume III 9; Tel. 971/72 73 40; fax 971/72 25 99.* A comfortable medium-sized and inexpensive hotel on a busy street in the very heart of Palma. 80 rooms. Major credit cards.

Hotel Meliá Confort Bellver €€€ *Paseo Ingeniero Gabriel Roca 11 (Passeig Marítim); Tel. 971/73 51 42; fax 971/73 14 51.* A large, modern, well-appointed hotel with restaurant and swimming pool situated in the center of the seafront in Palma. Popular with large groups. Wheelchair access. 389 rooms. Major credit cards.

West of Palma

Hotel Bon Sol €€€€ *Paseo de Illetas 30, Illetes; Tel. 971/40 21 11; fax 971/40 25 59.* A family-run, antique-filled hotel situated on multiple levels, cascading down the cliffs to its own secluded beach. Many other facilities including restaurant, sun terraces, and swimming pool. 92 rooms. Closed January. Major credit cards.

Hotel Brismar €-€€ *Almirante Riera Alemany` 6, Port d'Andratx; Tel. 971/67 16 00; fax 971/67 11 83.* A well-known and comfortable, if simple, seafront hotel located on the port's main drag. It's a bargain given the coveted location; request a room with a view of the harbor. Has a good family-style restaurant and terrace. Closed October–December. Wheelchair access. 56 rooms. Major credit cards.

Hotel Bendinat €€€€ *Urb. Bendinat (Portals Nous); Tel. 971/67 57 25; fax 971/67 72 76.* This mid-sized and handsome *hacienda*-style hotel is perched on a small, rocky cove. There are rooms with balconies and bungalows amid terraced gardens. Closed November–February. Wheelchair access. 31 rooms. Major credit cards.

Northwest Coast

Hotel Mar i Vent €€ *carrer Mayor 49, Banyalbufar; Tel. 971/61 80 00; fax 971/61 82 01.* Charming family-owned hotel atop a cliff with restaurant, terrace, and swimming pool. It has comfortable rooms and stunning views of the Mediterranean. A path leads to two quiet coves. Closed December–January. Breakfast and IVA included. 23 rooms.

Hotel Baronia € *carrer Mayor 49, Banyalbufar,; Tel. 971/61 81 46; fax 971/61 81 46.* Amid this tiny town's terraced groves is this endearingly simple and inexpensive hotel, which was originally part of a 17th-century Baronial tower. Rooms are a bit spartan, but all have terraces. Very attractive swimming pool. Closed November–April. 36 rooms.

Es Molí €€€€ *Ctra. Valldemossa-Deià, s/n, Deià; Tel. 971/63 90 00; fax 971/63 93 33; e-mail <esmoli@fehm.es>.* An elegant hotel in a converted 19th-century manor house on a hill, with incomparable views of the village and the sea. The pool is spring-fed, and the hotel's ensconced in 15,000 m^2 (18,000 sq. yds.) of private gardens. Rooms are very comfortable, and service, especially at breakfast on the terrace, is splendid. The highly recommended restaurant, Ca'n Quet, has its own gardens. Closed November–April. 87 rooms. Major credit cards.

Hostal C'Am Mario € *carrer Vetam 8, Valldemossa; Tel. 971/61 21 22.* This simple, pleasant, and old-fashioned *hostal* is conveniently situated in the center of Valldemossa and has its own restaurant serving good local food. 8 rooms. Major credit cards.

La Residencia €€€€ *Son Moragues, Deià; Tel. 971/63 90 11; fax 971/63 93 70; e-mail <laresidencia@atlas-iap.es>.* This elegant hotel, owned by Virgin's Richard Branson, is beautifully located in two 16th-century manor houses. Its chic international clientele enjoys full pampering: beauty and health center, beautiful pools, tennis courts, and El Olivo, one of the island's finest restaurants. 63 rooms. Major credit cards.

Hotel Costa D'Or €€ *Lluch Alcari s/n, Llucalcari; Tel. 971/63 90 25; fax 971/63 93 47; e-mail <costador@arrakis.es>.* A pleasant, comfortable hotel in an outstanding cliff-top setting overlooking the sea and mountains — an unparalleled setting for the affordable price. Full range of facilities, including restaurant, terraces, tennis court, and swimming pool with sea views. Directly across from the bus stop just outside of Deià. Reserve several months in advance. Breakfast included. Closed November–April. 42 rooms. Major credit cards.

Mallorca and Menorca

S'Hotel d'es Puig €€. *Es Puig, 4, Deià; Tel. 971/63 94 09; fax: 971/63 92 10; e-mail <puig@futurnet.es>.* Tucked away on the stone streets of tiny Deià is this delightful family-run *pension*. It has clean and hospitable rooms, a nice rooftop terrace, and pool. Relaxed and friendly. Closed mid-November–February. 8 rooms. Major credit cards.

Hostal Es Port €€ *Antonio Montis s/n, Port de Sóller; Tel. 971/63 16 50; fax 971/63 16 62.* An attractive hotel, one of the first in the area, with gardens, sun terraces, and a picturesque view over the port. Rooms are comfortable, but pale in comparison to the grounds. Situated close to the bus route and the train/tram service from Palma. Wheelchair access. 156 rooms.

Hotel El Guia € *Castanyer 2, Sóller; Tel. 971/63 02 27.* This pleasant, down-to-earth hotel offers excellent value. Nice courtyard and good restaurant. Near the train station. Closed November–April. 20 rooms.

Northeast

Hotel Formentor €€€€ *Platja de Formentor s/n, Formentor; Tel. 971/89 91 00; fax 971/86 51 55.* This classic hotel was inaugurated in 1929 — and it remains the only real development to date on incredible Formentor Peninsula. Guests have included film stars, world leaders, and business magnates. The garden terraces are spectacular, as are the beach and views. Rooms have charm, though they're a bit dated. Three swimming pools, three restaurants, full beauty center. Exclusivity doesn't come cheap. Closed mid-January–mid-February. 127 rooms. Major credit cards.

Hotel Niu €€€ *Cala Barcas, Cala Sant Vicenç; Tel. 971/53 01 00; fax 971/53 12 20; e-mail <hotel-niu@retemail.es>.* A pleasant, owner-managed and modern hotel overlooking the gorgeous coves of Cala Sant Vicenç. Simple facilities include terraces, bar, and restaurant. Reserve well in advance. Closed November–April. 24 rooms.

Cala Sant Vicenç €€€-€€€€ *carrer Maresers 2, Cala Sant Vicenç; Tel. 971/53 02 50; fax 971/53 20 84; <h.cala@pobox.com>*. It's hard to believe that this magnificently renovated, family-owned Relais & Chateaux property used to be a nondescript small hotel. Today it's both dignified and relaxed — small but with all the services and amenities of a large hotel, including an excellent restaurant and a pizzeria for the kids. Closed December–January. Wheelchair access. 38 rooms. Major credit cards.

Hotel Miramar €€ *Passeig Anglada Camarasa, 39, Port de Pollença; Tel. 971/86 64 00; fax 971/86 72 11; e-mail <h.miramar@fehm.es>*. A very comfortable beachfront hotel in family-friendly Port de Pollença. The terrace has magnificent views of the bay and Formentor. Some rooms have their own terraces. Closed–March. 80 rooms. Major credit cards.

Hotel Juma €€ *Plaça Major, 9, Pollença; Tel. 971/53 50 02; fax 971/53 41 55*. This small hotel, in a *Modernista* building right on Pollença's picturesque plaza, has been around since 1907. Rooms are very comfortably and charmingly old-fashioned. Plaza views are slightly more; breakfast included. Closed November–March. 8 rooms.

East & South Coasts

Hotel Cala d'Or €€-€€€ *Avinguda Belgica s/n, Cala d'Or; Tel. 971/65 72 49; fax 971/65 93 51*. Attractively situated amidst pine woods, this elegant but relaxed hotel overlooks a nearly private cove. The hotel has an established reputation; many guests return year after year. Rooms are comfortable and the staff friendly. Excellent facilities include swimming pool, terraces, restaurant, and beach bar. Excellent value. Breakfast buffet included. Closed November–February. 71 rooms. Major credit cards.

Hotel Ses Rotges €€ *Rafael Blanes 21, D.P. 0790, Cala Ratjada; Tel. 971/56 31 08; fax 971/56 35 81; e-mail <rotges@baleares.com>*. This small, very attractive and well-appointed hotel is in a quiet residential area close to the seafront. Owned and operated by a husband and wife, it's a quiet oasis in a busy resort area. The excellent restaurant has earned a Michelin star. Not suitable for children. Closed mid-November to mid-March. 24 rooms. Major credit cards.

Hotel Tres Playas €€€ *Cala Esmeralda, Colònia de Sant Jordi; Tel. 971/65 51 51; fax 971/65 56 44*. A modern and extremely well-appointed hotel set in its own garden overlooking the sea towards Es Trenc beach. There are rocks below the hotel, but a short path leads to the beach. Facilities include restaurant, swimming pool, and tennis court. Closed November–April. 118 rooms. Major credit cards.

Inland

Es Reco de Randa €€€-€€€€ *Font 13, Randa (4 km. from Algaida); Tel. 971/66 09 97, fax 971/66 25 58;e-mail <esreco@fehm.es>*. A delightful and intimate rural hotel in a Mallorcan manor house, in a village just east of Palma. Facilities include a swimming pool, sauna, and sun terrace, as well as an exceptional restaurant. The views are excellent. 14 rooms. Major credit cards.

Hostal de la Muntanya € *Ctra. Orient, km 10; Orient; Tel. 971/61 53 73*. A simple, rustic *hostal* in a quiet mountain village. Excellent value accommodation, and perfect for hikers who wish to tackle the surrounding mountains (including the Castell d'Alaró). Facilities include a restaurant and terrace for outdoor dining in fine weather. 13 rooms.

The Adventure Trail: Monasteries & Shelters

Santuari de Cura € *Puig de Randa, Algaida; Tel. 971/12 02 60 (reservations).* Basic and very economical accommodation in a tranquil location within easy access by road or on foot from Randa. Restaurant. Always fully booked in July and August.

Santuari de Lluc € *Monasteri de Lluc; Tel. 971/51 70 25; fax 971/51 70 25.* Simple but comfortable accommodation in a monastery that's Mallorca's most esteemed place of pilgrimage. The area is superb for walking. The monastery is accessible by road. Three restaurants, two bars, and two cafeterias; quiet hours are enforced after 11pm. Always fully booked in July and August.

MENORCA

Maó & Environs

Hotel del Almirante €-€€ *Carretera de Villacarlos, Maó; Tel. 971/36 27 00; fax 971/36 27 04; e-mail <hoTel.almirante@menorca.net>.* A nostalgic old hotel in a storied Georgian-style mansion that once belonged to Lord Collingwood. Attractive bedrooms and charming bar, plus garden and pool, on road between Maó and Es Castell. Excellent value. 40 rooms. Major credit cards.

Port Mahón €€€-€€€€ *Avinguda Fort de l'Eau 13, Maó; Tel. 971/36 26 00; fax 971/35 10 50.* An attractive Georgian-style mansion hotel, overlooking the harbor, and away from the center of Maó. Full range of facilities including swimming pool, terrace, bar, restaurant, and gardens. 82 rooms. Major credit cards.

Hostal Biniali €€-€€€ *Carretera S'uestra-Binibeca, 50; Tel. 971/15 17 24; fax 971/15 03 52.* A charming rustic hotel between Maó and the coves of the southeast coast, 1 km. from Sant Lluís. Attractively decorated rooms, recommended restaurant, and pool with country views. 20 rooms. Major credit cards.

Biniarroca Hotel Rural €€€-€€€€ *Carretera Sant Lluís-Es Castell; Tel. 971/15 00 59; fax 971/15 01 74.* This 16th-century farmhouse has been lovingly converted into an elegant country hotel, surrounded by ducks, sheep, geese, and donkeys. Rooms have period furniture and original art. Amenities include terrace bar, attractive pool, gardens, and restaurant. Breakfast included. 12 rooms. Major credit cards.

Fornells

Hostal Fornells €€ *carrer Major, 17; Tel. 971/37 66 76; fax 971/37 66 88; e-mail <fornells@chi.es>.* A modern and friendly small hotel in the attractive port of Fornells. Bills itself as a "health eco resort" offering a myriad of sports activities (mountain bikes for guests, diving, windsurfing, sailing, water skiing, golf, and exercise and nutrition programs). Small pool. Closed mid-October–April. 44 rooms. Major credit cards.

Ciutadella & Environs

Hotel Hespería Patricia €€-€€€ *Passeig Sant Nicolás 90-92, Ciutadella; Tel. 971/38 55 11; fax 971/48 11 20;website <www.hoteles-hesperia.es>.* A modern, well-appointed hotel in a quiet and enviable position overlooking the port of Ciutadella. Rooms are simple. Small pool. Closed mid-October–April. 44 rooms. Major credit cards.

Hotel Rural Sant Ignasi €€€-€€€€ *Carretera Cala Morell, Ciutadella; Tel. 971/38 55 75; fax 971/48 05 29; e-mail <santignasi@santignasi.com>.* Menorca's finest hotel, this charming rural property is equal parts rusticity and elegance. Just 4 km from Ciutadella in the middle of farm land, this 18th-century has been gorgeously restored and landscaped. Every room is different, though all are outfitted with period antiques; some have huge terraces, from which Mallorca is visible on a clear day. Excellent restaurant and inviting pool and bar; horseback riding. Breakfast buffet included. 20 rooms. Major credit cards.

Recommended Restaurants

You might not know it were you to stay tucked within a major coastal resort — where french fries seem to come with just about everything — but both islands have scores of authentic Spanish and Malllorcan/Menorcan restaurants frequented by locals and visitors interested in dining options more memorable than run-of-the-mill.

Anyone seeking good value should check out the *menú del día* — the daily fixed-price meal available at most restaurants — particularly at lunchtime. For about one-half the cost of ordering à la carte, you will be given three generous courses, including bread and wine or water. If you want to see the full menu, you request *la carta*.

As a basic guide, the symbols below indicate what you should expect to pay for a three-course meal for two, excluding wine, tax, and tip.

€	below 25 euros.
€€	25–50 euros.
€€€	50–75 euros.
€€€€	over 75 euros.

PALMA

Caballito del Mar €€ *Passeig de Sagrera 5; Tel. 971/72 10 74.* Open daily for lunch and dinner. The place to go for fresh fish and shellfish cooked to suit your own particular requirements. There's a delightful outside terrace — facing the waterfront and just around the corner from lively Plaça la Llotja — used for *al fresco* dining. Major credit cards.

Celler Sa Premsa € *Plaça Obispo Berenguer de Palou 8; Tel. 971/72 35 29.* Open for lunch and dinner; closed weekends. This Mallorcan dining hall is a real Palma institution and is very popular with foreigners. This is good, filling, everyday fare with a wide selection of Mallorcan classic dishes. The ambience is unbeatable and it's unbelievably inexpensive. Major credit cards.

Koldo Royo €€€ *Passeig Marítimo 3; Tel. 971/73 24 35.* Closed Saturday lunch and Sunday, the last week of January, first week of February, last week of June and first week of July. Considered by most to be Palma's best restaurant, this small and elegant place with one Michelin star overlooks the waterfront. It specializes in new-Basque cuisine. The menu is imaginative and unusual. Dishes include quail stuffed with rose petals and goose liver. Major credit cards.

Porto Pí €€€-€€€€ *Avda. Joan Miró, 174 y Garita, 25; Tel. 971/40 00 87.* Closed Saturday lunchtime and Sunday. Hidden away in the wrong end of town, by the port below Bellver Castle, this old Mallorcan house twinkles with a Michelin star. International dishes are prepared using fresh local ingredients and plenty of imaginative flair. An unforgettable gastronomic experience. Major credit cards.

La Bóveda €€ *Botería, 3; Tel. 971/71 48 63.* Open for lunch and dinner; closed Sunday. The foreigners line up outside the door every evening at 8pm, waiting hungrily for the door to slide open. But this lively tapas bar/restaurant is equally popular with locals—they just come later. The wide selection of tapas and main courses is uniformly excellent. Major credit cards.

Café Brondo €€ *carrer Brondo, 5; Tel. 971/71 55 67.* Open for lunch and dinner; closed Sunday. The top floor is a tapas bar; downstairs is a chic and intimate restaurant serving very creative Catalan and Mallorcan dishes with homemade desserts and a nice wine list; the house Ribera del Duero is also quite good. The lunch *menu del día* is an excellent deal.

Dalt Murada € *carrer Sant Roc, 1; Tel. 971/71 44 64.* Open for lunch and dinner; closed Sunday. In the heart of the old quarter, just a couple minutes from the cathedral, this atmospheric old noble house has a lovely garden — perfect for lunch or a summer's evening. A Mallorcan menu; the pre-fix lunch *menu* is a steal.

Ca'n Carlos €€ *carrer de s'Aigua, 5. Tel. 971/71 38 69.* Open for lunch and dinner; closed Sunday and second week of August. On a quiet pedestrian street, this charming place specializes in *cuina mallorquina*—Mallorcan cooking. Well-prepared dishes include roast lamb and eggplant stuffed with shellfish. Major credit cards.

West of Palma

Piazzeta € *Plaça Almirante Oquendo, 2, Port d'Andratx; Tel. 971/62 27 00.* Open daily for lunch and dinner. An extremely popular place just back from the port, serving good pizzas, pastas, and seafood. Resident ex-pats enjoy the attentive, friendly service. Major credit cards.

Tristán €€€-€€€€ *Puerto Punta Portals, Torre Capitanía, Portals Nous; Tel. 971/67 55 47.* Open for lunch and dinner; closed Mondays (though not May–September). Smart restaurant with two Michelin stars in this glamorous marina, with elegant outdoor dining and good views. Serves imaginative and attractive haute-cuisine dishes with a Mediterranean bent. Major credit cards.

Northwest Coast

Son Tomás €€ *Baronia 17, Banyalbufar; Tel. 971/61 81 49.* Open for lunch and dinner; closed Tuesdays and November–February. A small bar-restaurant with a terrace commanding outstanding views of the coast. Fresh fish comes directly from the boats in the cove; the *paella* and the *arroz negro* (black rice) are sumptuous. Major credit cards.

Ca'n Quet €€-€€€ *Crta. Valledemossa-Deià, Deià; Tel. 971/63 91 96.* Open for lunch and dinner; closed Monday and November–April. This renowned restaurant, overlooking Deià and associated with the fine hotel Es Molí, specializes in international cuisine with a unique local flavor. It's very popular with Mallorcans, who flock all the way from Palma for such delicacies as giant prawns wrapped in puff pastry.

El Olivo €€€-€€€€ *Son Canals, Deià; Tel. 971/63 90 11.* Open daily for dinner. For a special occasion, there's no better place than El Olivo, one of the top restaurants on the island. Delicious Mediterranean nouvelle cuisine is prepared under the watchful eye of the new French chef. It would be difficult to top dining on the terrace for sheer romance (though inside under the blazing candelabras comes close.) The wine cellar is one of the best in Mallorca. Daily tasting menu. Major credit cards.

Restaurant Jaime €€ *Archiduque Luis Salvador, 13, Deià; Tel. 971/63 90 29.* Open for lunch and dinner; closed Monday. Family-owned and -operated for more than three decades, this simple place — a nice contrast to the chic international restaurants that have sprouted in Deià — prepares generous helpings of authentic Mallorcan cooking. Look for fresh seafood and classics like *tumbet*. No coffee, though. (May be moving across the street next to Sa Dorada.) No credit cards.

El Guía €€ *Castanyer 3, Sóller; Tel. 971/63 02 27.* Open for lunch and dinner; closed Monday. In Sóller's nicest hotel, a small, well-run family restaurant that churns out Mallorcan home cooking, for which the perfect accompaniment is wine from Binissalem. Good-value *menu del día*. Major credit cards.

Es Guix € *Urbanizacion Es Guix Afueras Escorca s/n, Lluc; Tel. 971/51 70 92.* Closed Tuesday. A cool, green haven in the heat of the summer, this restaurant is equally inviting on cold winter days, when a log fire warms customers. Enjoy good Mallorcan home cooking on the beautiful terrace and take a dip in the restaurant's own private swimming pool. Always crowded weekends year-round. Major credit cards.

Bens D'Avall €€€ *Urbanització Costa Deià, Sóller; Tel. 971/63 23 81.* Open for lunch and dinner; closed Sunday night and Monday. A handsome, extremely personal restaurant on the coast between Deià and Sóller. A husband and wife team focus on seafood and Mallorcan specialties, and islanders come from Palma and Port d'Andratx on weekends. Major credit cards.

Northeast

Clivia €€ *Avinguda Pollentia, Pollença; Tel. 971/53 36 75.* Open for lunch and dinner; closed Tuesday lunch. This elegant and tranquil restaurant continues to grow in prestige. It's the perfect setting in which to enjoy chef Domingo García's original creations: Mallorcan cuisine is given a Basque flavor especially appreciated by local Spaniards. Here you'll taste perhaps the finest mussels on the island. Major credit cards.

Cavall Bernat €€€ *Maresers, Cala Sant Vicenç; Tel. 971/53 02 50.* Open daily for dinner; closed December–January. The former chef at Deià's prestigious El Olivo has created another island of fine dining, this time at a Relais & Chateaux hotel, the Cala Sant Vicenç. Refined Mediterranean cooking and a fine wine list. Major credit cards.

Restaurant Stay €€-€€€ *Muelle Nuevo s/n, Port de Pollença; Tel. 971/86 40 13.* Open for lunch and dinner; closed Monday and January–February. A smart, popular restaurant in the middle of the port, surrounded by bobbing boats. What else? The choice has to be fish, but there are also imaginative meat dishes. Good-value *menu del día,* also served at dinner. Highly recommended.

East Coast

Miramar € *Passeig Marítim, 2, Port de Alcúdia; Tel. 971/54 52 93.* Open daily for lunch and dinner. Miramar's been in business since 1871, and looking out to port, you can be sure the fish and shellfish are fresh. Highly recommended are the *arroz marinera* and *paella de mariscos.* Major credit cards.

Ses Rotjes €€€-€€€€ *Rafael Blanes 21, Cala Ratjada; Tel. 971/56 31 08.* Open daily for lunch and dinner; closed mid-November–mid-March.This French-owned *hostal* and restaurant with its Michelin star is a delightful find. The friendly husband-wife team is serious about fine dining, and every detail is cared for. If you want to know what that means, try the *menú gastronómico* — it's not cheap, but you'll definitely remember the experience. A regular local clientele testifies to the consistently high standard of cuisine; reservations are advised. Major credit cards.

Ca'n Trompé €-€€ *Avda. Bélgica, Cala d'Or; Tel. 971/65 73 41.* Open daily for lunch and dinner. The only authentic Mallorcan cookery in a sprawling and sophisticated resort along the southeast coast, but a very good one at that. Well-done dishes like *sopas mallorquinas* and stuffed zucchini at a fair price. Major credit cards.

Inland

Ses Porxeres €€-€€€ *Crta. Palma-Soller, km 17, Bunyola; Tel. 971/61 37 62.* Open for lunch and dinner; closed on Sunday evening, Monday, and August. A beautiful dining room near the historic gardens of Alfabia, this Catalan restaurant is justifiably famous in Mallorca. Specialties here include enormous appetizers, game, fish stews, and lamb cutlets grilled on hot rocks at your table. Reservations essential for Sunday lunch. Major credit cards.

Restaurante Mandala €€-€€€ *Orient; Tel. 971/61 52 85.* Open daily for lunch and dinner. In this rustic mountain hamlet there are only a couple hundred people but three good restaurants. This is the best, a family-run French eatery in an ancient stone house. The terrace is exceedingly romantic and the cooking creative. Major credit cards.

Celler C'an Amer €€ *carrer Pau, 39 Inca; Tel. 971/50 12 61.* Open daily for lunch and dinner; closed Sunday in summer and Monday, plus first half of July. This attractive and authentic *celler* — wine cellar — is renowned for excellent Mallorcan cooking, which makes imaginative use of seasonal ingredients. The place resonates with island ambience. The excellent house wine is their own. Major credit cards.

MENORCA

Pilar €€ *Forn, 61, Maó; Tel. 971/36 68 17.* Open for lunch and dinner; closed Sunday, Monday (off-season), January, and February. A husband-and-wife team is in charge of this personal and original restaurant, tops in Maó. The menu is diverse, fusing Menorcan dishes with Asian influences. Situated in a small, charming house in town. The *menú del día* is a good deal. Major credit cards.

Es Foquet € *Moll de Llevant 256, Maó; Tel. 971/35 00 58.* Open for lunch and dinner, closed mid-October–Easter. For some of the freshest seafood in the port, at excellent prices, this small place along the waterfront can't be topped. Interesting appetizers and homemade desserts. Major credit cards.

La Caraba €€ *S'uestrà, 78, Sant Lluís; Tel. 971/15 06 82.* Open daily for dinner; closed November to May. On the road from Sant Lluís to the coves of the southeast coast is this charming little white Menorca village house with a pretty terrace. The chef, Txema, prepares fresh, creative dishes, such as brochette of langoustines and dates wrapped in bacon, or breast of duck with dried peach sauce. There's a long list of interesting tapas, meant to be assembled as appetizers. Intimate and friendly, this is one of the most enjoyable restaurants in Menorca. Major credit cards.

Casa Manolo €€-€€€ *Marina 117-121, Port de Ciutadella; Tel. 971/38 00 03.* Open daily for lunch and dinner; closed November. One of the most popular of the seafood restaurants clamoring for tourists' attention along the port, Manolo is a friendly, family-run place that has aimed to please for more than 40 years. From clams to *caldereta de langosta*, it specializes in a wide choice of freshly caught fish. Major credit cards.

Racó d'es Palau €-€€ *carrer d'es Palau, 3, Ciutadella; Tel. 971/38 54 02.* Open daily for lunch and dinner. This simple restaurant is hidden down one of the atmospheric streets of old Ciutadella, a minute from the cathedral. Friendly and inviting, it's perfect for pizzas, pastas, and also fresh fish and shellfish at reasonable prices. Major credit cards.

Es Molí des Raco €€ *Vicario Fuxa 53, Es Mercadal; Tel. 971/37 53 92.* Open daily for lunch and dinner. An attractive country-style restaurant set in an old mill with a pleasant terrace for summer dining. Always a good *menu del día*. Specialties include stuffed vegetables and traditional Menorcan dishes. Reservations essential for evening dining during the high season. Major credit cards.

Es Pla €€-€€€ *Passaig Es Pla, Fornells; Tel. 971/37 66 55.* Open daily for lunch and dinner. The port of Fornells is known for its fine fish restaurants, and this one, which has been around for 35 years, is one of the most popular with locals. It's right on the water. The baked fish and authentic *caldereta de langosta* are highly recommended. Major credit cards.

INDEX